GuitarPlayer

PRESENTS

50

UNSUNG HEROES OF THE GUITAR

D1128938

Guitar Player

PRESENTS

50

UNSUNG HEROES OF THE GUITAR

EDITED BY MICHAEL MOLENDA

Backbeat Books

An Imprint of Hal Leonard Corporation

Portions of this book are adapted from articles that originally appeared in *Guitar Player* magazine.

Published in cooperation with Music Player Network, New Bay Media, LLC, and *Guitar Player* magazine. *Guitar Player* magazine is a registered trademark of New Bay Media, LLC.

Published in 2011 by Backbeat Books
An Imprint of Hal Leonard Corporation
7777 West Bluemound Road
Milwaukee, WI 53213

Trade Book Division Editorial Offices
33 Plymouth St.
Montclair, NJ 07042

Printed in the United States of America

All text content courtesy of *Guitar Player* magazine/New Bay Media, except articles by Lowell Cauffiel, Dan Forte, Stefan Grossman, Lee Hildebrand, Jimmy Leslie, Steve Rosen, and Jon Sievert, used by permission.

Every reasonable effort has been made to contact copyright holders and secure permissions. Omissions can be remedied in future editions.

Photo credits: Hollywood Fats © Clayton Call; Tommy Bolin © Steve Caraway; John Sykes © Rick Gould; Earl Slick © Richard Johnson/Camera Press/Retna Ltd.; Terry Kath © Andrew Kent/Retna Ltd.; David Torn © Jonnie Miles/Retna Ltd.; James Williamson © Michael Ochs Archive/Getty Images; Charlie Baty, Lenny Breau, Rory Gallagher © Jon Sievert; Carrie Brownstein and Corin Tucker © Robert Spencer/Retna Ltd. All other images courtesy of *Guitar Player* magazine.

Book design by Damien Castaneda

Library of Congress Cataloging-in-Publication Data is available upon request.

ISBN 978-1-61713-021-2

www.backbeatbooks.com

CONTENTS

EDITOR'S NOTE

THIS BOOK WAS INSPIRED BY ONE OF THOSE "IDIOTIC" IDEAS
of the *Guitar Player* staff—to pay homage to 101 "Forgotten Greats and Unsung Heroes" in the magazine's February 2007 issue. It wasn't that the *concept* was foolish, thank goodness, but trying to compile, evaluate, select, reevaluate, finalize, research, write, and copyedit a piece on 101 guitarists of *any* stature became a Herculean task that threatened to obliterate the deadline demands of a monthly publication. Many heads exploded, and several ulcers raged, but we got it done.

Then, of course, we had to sit back and await the banshee wails and vicious attacks of readers who didn't agree with each and every one of the staff's 101 choices. Hey, no good deed goes unpunished, right?

But, to employ yet another apt cliché, "time is a great healer," and we've come to value and celebrate the blitzkriegs of impassioned commentary we trigger with our frequent big-list issues such as "The 50 Greatest Guitar Tones of All Time," "The 50 Most Influential Rock Solos Ever," and "50 Forgotten Albums Every Guitarist Should Own."

After all, the primary mission of *Guitar Player* is helping guitarists of all styles and ages and skill levels to sound better and play better. Doing that gig with sincerity and credibility and love means that, occasionally, you must churn things up a bit, and nothing whips up a tumult of outcry like a list that may or may not include someone's favorite guitar hero.

The good side of these debacles—the really, really terrific and wonderful good side—is that obsessed guitarists absolutely disagree on certain selections, and then they share their *own* picks with other players via online forums, Facebook, Twitter, and letters to the editors of *Guitar Player*. They also scatter their opinions at gigs and bars and coffee joints and rehearsal halls and wherever musicians hang out. The community dialog becomes much bigger than the thing itself—the original article or book—and the satellite debates serve to turn on players to even more guitarists they may otherwise have never heard about. The genius of meaningful provocation is that it can drive people to discover more. In fact, *your* next orgy of discovery might even start from this very book.

How did a player come to be one of this volume's "50 unsung" guitarists? Well, first, each of the 50 had to be a *musical force*. You might not be totally into the style one of them plays, but we're hoping you'll always learn something valuable from his or her technique, tone, note choices, experimentalism, pop sense, and/or attitude.

Second, they had to be somewhat off the current guitar-hero radar. Terry Kath, for example, was in one of the biggest groups of the '70s (Chicago), but he is seldom name-checked today. We also made the decision to include some formidable women players in our "unsung" list, because, in whatever era they performed, they were likely not afforded the same prominence as male guitarists of their time. A sad cultural note.

Finally—and this is the most subjective and dangerous aspect of the criteria—we tried to assess that if whatever environmental elements preventing these 50 guitarists from becoming popular heroes were removed from the equation, would their talents alone steer their ascension to the iconic stature of a Clapton, Page, Hendrix, Beck, SRV, or Van Halen? No way to answer that one based on irrefutable evidence, of course, but it was a blast hypothesizing the impossible.

So there you have it—our list of 50 "unsung heroes." I invite you to celebrate them, dispute them, study them, and learn from them. As with other *Guitar Player Presents* series books, the interviews and stories for each of the 50 players have been pulled from the *GP* archives (1967 to the present), and we've noted whether the original magazine content is complete or excerpted.

At this point, I want to give special thanks to the staffs—past and present—of *Guitar Player*. Since 1967, these editors and writers have always sought to challenge, entertain, educate, and excite everyone who loves those crazy planks of wood and steel. Their talents are mammoth, and their evangelism has had a profound effect on the guitar community of today. Bravo! I must also launch a major shout-out to the ever-patient Bernadette Malavarca and her Backbeat Books crew, who never get these manuscripts when they want them, but nonetheless work miracles with many threads of diverse content to deliver compelling reads. And, of course, Cheryl, Iggy, mom, and all my family members and great friends keep me sane, amused, frightened, and well loved as I lurch through my earthly tenure.

Michael Molenda
Editor in Chief, *Guitar Player*
June 2011

GuitarPlayer

PRESENTS

50
UNSUNG HEROES OF THE GUITAR

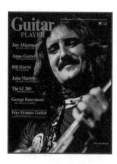

Jan Akkerman

BY STEVE ROSEN | MAY 1975

JAN AKKERMAN, LEAD GUITARIST OF FOCUS, REPRESENTS the new breed of European guitarists so long invisible under the veil of the English players. Where the islander tends to base his playing more on the American blues scene and his own contemporaries (legends such as Jeff Beck, Eric Clapton, and Jimmy Page), the continental devotee has influences as far afield as J. S. Bach and Django Reinhardt. Because the European musician tends to be a bit more eclectic in his approach to the instrument, it has taken this country longer to accept him within the ranks of the straight British and American rock guitarists. Jan Akkerman's technique and tone quality combine the subtlety and demand of the classical guitar (on which he is highly accomplished) with the roar and tenacity of the electric instrument.

What was your first real work with a band?

I guess it was the Friendship Sextet. These guys were 21, 23, and I was 10. But this was just on the weekends, because these guys kept asking my parents, "Hey, he should play with us." But my parents said, "No, this boy isn't going to go anywhere." So I started playing in nightclubs and in the first rock shows in Holland about 16 years ago. We were already playing rhythm and blues, Buddy Holly, Fats Domino— stuff like that. I started listening to the radio about this time for as much as I could, because I didn't have a record player.

When did the band Brainbox happen?

That was about '68, and was a good deal after the Sextet. I had a bad name in Holland because I'd run from group to group. I went to nightclubs without my parents knowing it and sat in with the bands. Kind of a "guitarophile." Brainbox was kind of hard rock—something like Bad Company—though the sound Bad Company gets is much better than what we got. I was using a Gretsch White Falcon, a Cordovox Leslie, and a self-made amp. I didn't know how to make one—I just did it. It had two speakers, and I had the Leslie miked up through two Elco speakers.

They were Italian speakers with the big ducts for the high tones. I miked that up stereo. You have three wheels turning around in the Cordovox—one on the bottom, one in the middle, and one on top. I was really into that, having the whole stage with cabinets like that, and the sound turning all around like a rainbow.

What was the guitar scene like in Amsterdam?

Oh, jazz, jazz. We never listened to English guitar players, except maybe the Shadows and Clapton. I was into jazz and rock and roll. When I heard somebody like Beck or Clapton playing, they just dated what I was already doing. I was doing it before them, as simple as that. The sound of Clapton was always beautiful, brilliant, but I was listening to Django Reinhardt, Tal Farlow, Bola Sete, Julian Bream, and Larry Coryell.

Do you think your playing is more jazz influenced now?

No, I've stayed a rock player, but with another choice of notes—European maybe. I do play different from all guitar players I've heard. Of course, one person always plays different from another. I'm different rhythmically, technically, and harmonically, and also mentally. I'm a technical player from what I hear around me, but just technique is not my trip. It's musical technique. Like playing beautiful things, but also technically perfect. I'm not talking about speed, because I have that also very much—I'm talking about tone. About getting the tone out with the right amount of brilliance, the right attack of the pick, the right vibrato.

"I'm a technical player from what I hear around me, but just technique is not my trip. It's musical technique."

What type of guitar are you using now?

It's an old Les Paul. I've had everything taken off, and I've had maple overlaid on the body. I think it's a '70 or a '71. It's not that old. It doesn't have to be necessarily old for a good guitar—you just have to do your own thing with it. I put in new frets that are square against the fretboard. I don't like the frets when they're rounded because it's too difficult to play the way I play. The neck has been flattened and also the action, because it was too round. With these square frets a bit high up and the neck flattened, it gives a better tone. It's more in pitch, and it plays easier. I've put on those German tuning pegs, Schaller, but I like Grovers a lot. I've also had the pickups rewired so they get more treble. I use more treble than maybe any other guitar player I know. The strings should be pulled and not drawn down to the body, because it takes away the sustain. I use Ernie Ball—they're the best—gauged .008, .011, .014, .022, .030, and .038. They are really thin strings, but I like it like that because you have to play very clean on it—very secure like on a violin. You have to have the perfect touch.

Have you ever tried using a Fender if you like that treble sound?

Sometimes I did, but it's not my guitar. I still want to get that belly sound—that fat "oomph" with the brilliance on top. A real screaming sound that goes through your bones.

Why did you design your own guitar for Framus?

As a rock guitarist, I always liked to play a big hollowbody guitar, but I couldn't, just because of the feedback. But on the Framus, since the neck runs through the entire length of the guitar, it doesn't feed back. The shape I kept between the Les Paul model and a hollowbody. The neck is wider at the top, so bending strings in lower positions is easier. The head is shaped concisely, so the strings don't touch each other, and they can ring without interference.

You use a unique setup for amplification.

I'm developing now a new kind of approach in using amps. I'm using Crowns as slave amps and a preamp—totally studio equipment. I also use six Leslies with high-powered JBL speakers, two big Fender solid-state amps, and Fender cabinets loaded with four 10" JBLs. On the Leslies, I've switched systems. I've taken the amps out and driven them directly into the speakers for better sound quality. The Crowns are really powerful. I use two, stereo, so that's four times 600 watts. I like having that much power.

Do you feel you're able to achieve all you want to through Focus?

Yes, I do. Focus is, for me, one of the few groups who know how to catalyze love for music and voice. We get into the theatrics strictly through the music—like with "Hocus Pocus." I wouldn't take my guitar off or anything like that, but for the people that do, it's okay. I don't know what that has to do with guitar playing, but everybody has to make his own way up to heaven, I guess.

Geographically, the guitar is a very difficult instrument. A piano is all before you. On guitar, you have these strange scales, and you have this one hand to make bass and melody and accompany, and that's really difficult.

I've got my own hangups about the guitar. If people didn't like my playing, that wouldn't be an excuse to quit. That would be alright. That's not what I'm looking for. I want to reach the people with pure beauty. I want to make pure music. I may be the only one looking in that direction. I'm not sure. There's no one else I can think of. I told you I'm an ego-tripper, but for the people. I feel I've got responsibility to the instrument in the first place. If you have a gift, you have to do something with it or for it. I work. I'm a laborer. What more can I tell you? *—Excerpted from the May 1975 issue of* Guitar Player

Davie Allan

BY ART THOMPSON | JANUARY 1996

"I'VE BEEN TOLD I SOUND LIKE DUANE EDDY WITH DIRTY fingernails," says B-movie 6-stringer Davie Allan. "I'm the mellowest person around, but when I put on a guitar, I become a wild man."

Throughout the late '60s, Davie Allan and the Arrows' garage-surf instrumentals set the beat for dozens of late-'60s motorcycle-gang-terror films, such as *Born Losers*, *Devil's Angels*, *Wild in the Streets*, *Thunder Alley*, and *The Glory Stompers*. Though the Arrows were America's number-one instrumental rock band in '67, their success fizzled by the end of the decade. Thanks in part to the recent Iloki release of *Loud, Loose, and Savage*, however, Allan's tough, rangy, fuzz-soaked guitarwork is getting some long-overdue respect.

"Seeing Elvis on TV as a kid inspired me to get into music, but Nokie Edwards of the Ventures, Duane Eddy, and Link Wray were my main influences," says Davie. "In high school in '65, I met a guy named Mike Curb [later to become California's lieutenant governor], who got the Arrows going with a song called 'Blue's Theme.' Roger Corman used it in his '67 movie *The Wild Angels*, and it became a single. From then until '69, we did about two dozen flicks—mostly biker and marijuana-type things."

Allan played in Top 40 and oldies bands throughout the '70s and '80s, worked in a radio station, and briefly re-formed the Arrows in '82. The band's full recovery came in '93. Though he originally twanged his Mosrite guitar through a Mosrite fuzz, a

Vox wah, and a Fender Concert amp, Davie's current weapons of choice include a '65 Fender Jazzmaster feeding a Roland GP-8 effects processor and a Music Man RD-100 amp.

"I've been told I sound like Duane Eddy with dirty fingernails."

"I put Duncan pickups in the Jazzmaster and changed the bridge, and I'm also using a ProCo Rat pedal," he details. "With my amp cranked and the fuzz on 10, the noise is as loud as the notes."

With newest Arrows Dave Provost on bass and David Winogrond on drums, Allan says he's ready to rock.

"We've recorded three new songs for an upcoming album, and Roger Corman recently used 'Invasion of the Body Surfers' for a TV movie called *Not Like Us*. It has been almost 30 years since he last used us—now we're a bunch of old men playing nasty punk music."

Jennifer Batten

BY JOE GORE | JULY 1989

"WOMEN ARE THE WEAKER SEX. A WOMAN'S PLACE IS IN
the home. Women can't be president because they're too emotional. It's a man's
world. I remember hearing phrases like these when I was growing up," recalls Jennifer Batten. "But when I was a teenager, my sister told me that there were no differ-
ences between men and women apart from the physical, and I held that statement
in the back of my mind whenever self-doubt would arise."

Listen up, guys—and, most likely, you *are* a guy. Ninety-eight percent of *Guitar
Player* subscribers are male, a higher figure than for *Playboy* or *Penthouse*. You may be
less likely to hear blanket statements about women's aptitude for guitar playing than
in the past—although such Cro-Magnon attitudes persist in some quarters—but
there are still "No Girls Allowed" signs posted outside the rock-guitar clubhouse.
Record labels that can't comprehend female musicians unless they fall into one of a
few permissible categories, rock videos that are more likely to feature men who look
like women than actual women, music ads designed to cater to the sex and power
fantasies of teenage boys—they're all part of the cockeyed world of rock guitar.

Sure, the music business is tough for everybody. But for a female instrumentalist
to succeed, she must have all the requisite talent and persistence, *plus* the strength to
go against the thousands of little signals that mediate against that success. Jennifer
Batten is just such a musician.

As a lead guitarist for Michael Jackson's latest world tour, Batten performed before literally millions of listeners. She has taught at Hollywood's Guitar Institute of Technology (GIT) and authored a number of instructional books and columns. Her unique approach to two-handed tapping technique integrates elements of blues, metal, classical, and jazz, but she's no slouch at conventional-style playing, either.

Born in upstate New York, Batten took up the guitar at eight.

"I remember seeing the Beatles on *The Ed Sullivan Show* and thinking they were the coolest thing in the world," she says. "My dad played a little, so there was already a guitar in the house. My sister got a guitar before I did, and I was jealous. I was determined to get one real quick."

A year later, her family moved to California. Jennifer has played continuously since then, but she didn't start working with bands until she graduated from GIT in 1979.

"I wouldn't consider myself a shredder, but I think that's something important to have in your playing."

"My mother wouldn't let me go to strange places at night," she recalls, "so I had to play along with records at home."

She soon made up for lost time, however, playing for dozens of musical projects in an unlikely array of styles and administering guitar lessons to a small army of would-be shredding machines.

You've done quite a bit of genre jumping in your career.

Yeah, I guess you could say I'm pretty schizophrenic. But a lot of it had to do with my teachers. I had lessons since I started. At first, I was into pop, like the Monkees and the Dave Clark Five. Then I hooked up with a folk teacher, so that's what I learned. Later, he went on tour, so I ended up studying with a guy who was into blues, so I got into that bag—Howlin' Wolf, B. B. King, and John Lee Hooker. When I was 12 or 13, my father took me to see Sonny Terry and Brownie McGhee, and it was great. And my dad played some guitar, so he turned me on to Django Reinhardt and Charlie Christian. I thought it was great stuff. When I enrolled in GIT, my favorite guitarists were Duane Allman and B. B. King. But then I started studying with Joe Diorio and Ron Eschete, and I turned into a little jazz Nazi. I got to the point where I hated rock. I thought it was really moronic. I put on records that I used to love, and I just hated them. It was really a strange space to be in. Later, I joined my first full-time band, Purl. They had been doing a fusion thing, but right after I joined, they decided to go rock. So I eventually got back into it and put my jazz Nazi days behind me.

How did you get involved in two-handed tapping?

Steve Lynch was in my class at GIT in '79. After he saw an Emmett Chapman

seminar on the Stick, he started experimenting with the same technique on standard guitar. It sounded great to me. I had to follow him at the graduation performance, which was a drag, because he whipped out all this stuff that just fried people's minds. It was so fresh and new then, and nobody had seen it before. Eddie Van Halen was just coming on the scene, and I don't think people in the class were even aware of what he was doing at the time.

I corresponded with Steve after school, and he gave me a demo tape of his two-handed stuff. I had trouble picking things out because I was using only the index finger of my right hand. But when his book, *The Right Touch*, came out, I tore through it and learned everything in it. Later, I started experimenting on my own, and eventually I took a completely different direction. But that book really helped me understand some of the things that could be done with the technique. By that point, I was studying Eddie Van Halen's stuff, and I was into everyone who was using the technique, so I learned solos by Eddie, Randy Rhoads, Jeff Watson, and even Adrian Vandenberg—who played some twohanded background parts on one of his first solo albums.

Fairly or unfairly, tapping technique came to be identified with Eddie Van Halen. Did you ever feel that there were certain Eddie-isms that you had to avoid in order to develop your own sound?

Yeah. A lot of people started doing those repeated triplet figures like Eddie plays on "Eruption," so I tried to stay away from that. One way I avoided it was by experimenting with using all four right-hand fingers.

You often generate unusual harmonies by tapping with two or three fingers simultaneously.

Tapping lets you get chord clusters that you couldn't get otherwise. It's like Allan Holdsworth for short fingers! You can play all those chords that hurt.

What are the relative merits of tapping technique and conventional technique for improvising?

For me, it's a bit easier to pick over changes than to tap. But a lot of rock stuff is based in one key, anyway.

Can being perceived as a "two-handed player" be a limitation?

I'm sure people do categorize me like that, but I don't think of it as a limitation. For me, two-handed playing is like going to another instrument. Some guitar players write at the piano because it's a fresh approach. I think of the two-handed stuff the same way. It lets you see the neck differently, and you can come up with fresh ideas that you might not have otherwise.

You've done quite a bit of teaching yourself. What did that bring to your playing?

It paid the rent! But teaching can enhance what you know and make it more solid in your mind. I've had students who would really push me or force me to get into bags that I might otherwise not have gotten into.

Did you work on reading with all your students?

I tried. Guitar players are probably the worst readers in the world. Most of them didn't start out by reading, and guitar is just a tough instrument to read on, unlike, say, a saxophone, which only has one middle *C*. I'm not a Tommy Tedesco-type reader, but reading was always a part of my education since I was eight. But if a student really didn't want to do it, that was cool, too. Some great players don't read at all. Warren Di Martini says he plays completely by ear, but he sounds great. Same with Jeff Beck. Allan Holdsworth can't read, and most guitarists would die for his chops. Art can't be a regimented thing.

In general, are there some areas that students focus on too heavily?

Well, all the teenage boys who came in wanted one thing—to shred. They weren't interested in getting the foundations together. I'd try to present it in little doses, so it wouldn't hurt. Music teaching is totally a giving profession, and sometimes you don't get anything back. With some students, I would give, give, give, and they would come back next week without using anything that I had shown them. But with some students, it's very exciting to see how they progress and to think that maybe someday they'll be sharing a bill with you.

You've also played for a lot of musical projects, including some fairly weird ones.

I played with a gospel singer named Ella Ruth Piggee—that was her real name. I played in [singer] Lydia Van Houston's heavy metal band. I never had to use a clean sound all night—it was just full-out blasting on 10. I think I damaged some ears. I played in Girlfriend, a straight-ahead R&B band put together by Narada Michael Walden. In Doc Tahri, we did some pretty fun experimental things, like playing random arpeggios over a stupid unison groove while the drummer sang "Roxanne." We lost a few people, but at least I was entertained. And I toured the South Pacific with a hairdresser/Elvis impersonator. But that's all history, as they say. Now I'm concentrating on preparing my record.

What will it be like?

It will be a mostly instrumental rock guitar album. You know, 24 tracks, 19 of them guitar [*laughs*]. There will be a minimum of vocals. It will be kind of a metallish thing. I wouldn't want to do any lightweight Jacuzzi jazz. Michael Sembello is producing. A lot of people only know him from his hit song, "Maniac," but he's a very good guitarist. He played with Stevie Wonder for seven years. He has produced mainly R&B artists, like George Benson and Chaka Khan. My album won't be like that, but there are a lot of things that I really like about R&B production, like the breakdowns, the different textures, and the giant drum sounds.

How much material will be original?

About half. I'd like to do Coltrane's "Giant Steps" and "Naima," and I'd like to use "Flight of the Bumblebee" as an intro or something. I might even do a metal ballad—even though I usually hate them. I wish I could find an electronic ballad remover for my records.

You've managed to succeed in a very male-dominated profession. Why do you think there are so few prominent women guitarists?

It's partly because there's no precedent. Maybe a lot of boys coming up can really identify with all the rockers they see on MTV or at concerts. When I was coming up, there were only a few women soloists, like Emily Remler. But I think that things will be completely different in the 1990s. More girls are enrolling in GIT, for example, and you hear about women players all the time. And if I can influence people in that way, it's great.

Some stereotypes die hard.

I don't have much patience with stereotypes or generalizations of any kind. One of the biggest stereotypes about women is that they are "too emotional." But isn't music pure emotion? If that's the case, there should be 2 percent males in music and 98 percent women. A lot of downers like these are seeded into people's minds. I'm sure I don't even recognize half of the little seeds that were planted in my mind as I was growing up.

During the Michael Jackson tour, I thought about this a lot. I read *The Cinderella Complex* by Colette Dowling. She talks about how some women get trapped into thinking they should just get through school, and then they'll meet Prince Charming. I have a lot of respect for women who raise a family—that can be tougher than any career, with years and years of sacrifice. But I think some women who might have gone into music went that way instead. Perhaps that's one reason there aren't so many women in the music workforce. I mean, it's still a shock for some people to see a woman playing the guitar. All over the world, on the Michael Jackson tour, people would ask me whether I was a man or a woman. Just because I played guitar, they assumed I was a guy.

Is it possible that some of our concepts of "good guitar playing" are excessively male? What about the image of the guitar hero/gunslinger or the excessive emphasis on technique?

Well, I'm still into chops—I can appreciate that as much as the next guy. I wouldn't consider myself a shredder, but I think that's something important to have in your playing. But the gunslinger attitude is pretty jive. The whole competitive thing gets really old, because it gets so far away from the art of music. If you have chops, they'll say you have no soul. If you play blues, they'll say you have no chops. If you play jazz, you're too old. If you play punk, you're an idiot. I've been there myself, and I've done the slagging. When I was at GIT, I was slagging the rockers. Being with Michael Jackson, I could really see what the slag scene was about. He sold 40 million copies of *Thriller* and 20 million copies of *Bad*. He's the most beloved entertainer in the world, yet reviewers constantly shredded him to bits.

How did you land the audition for his band?

I heard about it from Steve Trovato, a guitarist friend of mine. I tried to set up the audition for the latest possible date so I could stay home and shred Michael Jackson tunes night and day. The actual audition was by myself in front of a video camera. They said they wanted to hear some funk rhythms, so that's what I started out with. Then I went into solo land. I played my solo version of John Coltrane's "Giant Steps," and then I played the "Beat It" solo—which I'd been playing for years in Top-40 bands. I had heard they wanted a certain look, but I'd never paid much attention to how I looked before. I'm not into that at all.

When I got the call saying that they wanted me, they asked me two questions: "Can you tour for a year?" and "Do you mind an image change?" I said, "Do what you want," so when the tour started in Japan, I had a three-foot Mohawk. Michael had hired a designer who made drawings of how everyone was supposed to look before we even started rehearsing. The drawings looked great, but in real life, we were some ugly people onstage!

How long did you rehearse before the tour?

For six weeks. It was the most intense rehearsal I've ever done. Every nuance was worked out—mostly before we even met Michael. Sometimes we worked for 12 hours a day. The choreographer, Vince Patterson, had worked out all the moves in advance, and he knew better than to try to make us dance while we played. [Keyboardist/arranger] Greg Phillinganes was the musical director, and he has the most incredible ears. We rehearsed at mega dBs, and if just one vocal part was off for one note in the third bar, he'd hear it and remember it. Michael had suggestions for people, and he was very cool to work with. He has unbelievable patience and a low stress level. He never raised his voice once during the entire tour. After the tour started, we hardly saw him at all. But a couple of times we all closed down amusement parks together. That's the only way to see Tokyo Disneyland, man.

One of your spotlights was the "Beat It" solo. Did you play Eddie Van Halen's original solo note-for-note?

Yeah. Backstage at Madison Square Garden, [bassist] Will Lee asked me if it was on tape! I guess it was a back-handed compliment, but it made me wonder how many people thought it was on tape. As I played, I was wearing a fiber-optic suit that changed colors, and so did the guitar. I had to put glow-in-the-dark tape on the neck to mark the frets so I wouldn't get lost. Lights were flashing, so it was like moving through a strobe-lit disco. A few times, somebody stepped on the cord that connected my suit to the computer, and I almost got whiplash. I'd played the solo for years, but with Michael it was more challenging because the tempo was faster than the record, and the guitars were tuned down two whole steps to C for that song, so I had to use heavy-gauge strings. Plus, I had to move around and jump up and down. I usually stand still when I solo.

Eventually, I got to play the solo for Eddie Van Halen. Eddie happened to be in the next room at a rehearsal studio, working on some stuff with his technicians. He'd heard that I played his solo on the tour, and he wanted me to play it for him. Not the most relaxed situation for me! He had me play his red and white 5150 guitar, and then he asked me to show the solo to him, because he'd forgotten it. —*Excerpted from the July 1989 issue of* Guitar Player

Charlie Baty

BY ART THOMPSON | AUGUST 2002

FOR MORE THAN 25 YEARS, LITTLE CHARLIE & THE NIGHTCATS
have kept the blues scene invigorated with fur-flying performances that showcase
the explosive guitar playing of Charlie Baty. Baty began his career as a harmonica
player, only picking up guitar to learn some classic blues licks to teach his 6-string-
playing friends. It wasn't until he and vocalist/harpist Rick Estrin formed the Nightcats in 1976 that Baty started playing guitar full time.

"I knew a little about nothing" is how Baty describes his abilities at the time.

By 1982, when the Sacramento, California-based band released its debut album,
All the Way Crazy, the members had become high-energy performers who used blues
as a launching pad to explore swing, jazz, rockabilly, and even gospel.

"We wanted people to dance," says Baty, "so we did whatever we could to help round
out our show. Back in the '80s, we were one of the few bands to mix Chicago-style blues
with stuff that had more of a swing beat. We were going for an older sound at a time
when a lot of guys were trying to be Stevie Ray Vaughan or the Fabulous Thunderbirds."

Though his multifaceted style echoes T-Bone Walker, Buddy Guy, Luther Tucker,
and Kenny Burrell, Baty cites jazz-guitar pioneer Charlie Christian as his primary
influence.

"Christian was sort of a Rosetta Stone for me," he says. "He opened up my ears
to phrasing, and he gave me ideas about making the jump between blues and swing.
I didn't just cop his licks, though—I wanted to understand how he played over the

standards of his time. I can read music, and that helped me visualize what was going on harmonically with his solos. I've also studied [saxophonist] Charlie Parker's approach to solos, as compared to someone like Little Walter. They both play beautiful ideas, but they go about it in entirely different ways."

Baty's guitars include '57 and '66 Stratocasters, a pair of reissue Strats (a '57 and a '62), a Fender Swingmaster (a Tele-style hollowbody with a bird's-eye maple top and three P-90s), a Gibson ES-295 (his main road guitar), and a 1949 Gibson ES-5 equipped with three P-90s.

"That was the first jazz guitar I owned, and it has this cool, western-swing kind of sound," he says. "When I bought it in the '70s, I was told it had been owned by a western-swing guitarist who lived in the Sacramento area. I like to think that might have been Junior Bernard [of the Texas Playboys]. A name had been inlaid on the original fingerboard, but it had been replaced with a plain ebony board when I got it."

"I come up with my best stuff onstage."

Baty's strings are fairly heavy—.011–.050 sets on the Fenders and .012–.052 or .013–.056 sets on the Gibsons—and he uses heavy picks. A blackface Super Reverb is his main stage amp, but he occasionally uses a Vero Paramount 4x10 combo. In the studio, he might rev up one of three vintage Fenders: a '55 Pro, a 1x15 Vibroverb, and a Vibrosonic.

"I don't haul those old amps out on the road," says Baty, "so getting to use stuff I don't play all the time is the fun part of making records."

Baty installs new-old-stock Phillips 6L6 output tubes in his Super Reverb, and he credits amp-tech Skip Henderson for showing him how biasing can affect tone.

"My main Super is biased more like a Fender Pro," says Baty, "which gives it a thick distortion at a fairly low volume. I don't like to crank my amp up until it starts sounding like a fuzzbox. Also, I used to blow the old Jensen speakers in my Super pretty regularly, so I replaced them with a set of Eminence ceramic-magnet 10s. I've been using those speakers for quite a while now without any problems, and they have better bass response than the Jensens."

Playing some 200 shows a year leaves the Nightcats little time for recording, but when they do get in the studio, the band strives for a spontaneous live vibe.

"I come up with my best stuff onstage," assesses Baty. "I've never been all that comfortable in the studio. It's hard not to feel the pressure of having to be creative right now. I don't like to overdub solos, so if I make a mistake, we do another take or I just live with it. After doing this for 25 years, I've realized that I'm never going to be as good as I'd like. All I can do is keep practicing and keep learning."

Robbie Blunt

BY JAS OBRECHT | OCTOBER 1985

AFTER MORE THAN A DECADE AS A JOURNEYMAN MUSICIAN
for various British bands, Robbie Blunt scored the prized position of guitarist and co-songwriter for Robert Plant, the former lead singer of Led Zeppelin. His work on Plant's three solo albums is wide-ranging and sophisticated, leaning more toward tasty understatement than flash. Perhaps the most distinctive earmark of Robbie's playing on *Pictures at Eleven* and *The Principle of Moments* is the crystal-clear tone of his '50s Strat, which is best epitomized on the hit "Big Log." Blunt retired his favorite Strat for the recently issued *Shaken 'N' Stirred*, using instead a Roland guitar synthesizer and a newer, customized Strat that enabled him to expand his use of the tremolo arm.

Robbie was born and raised in Kidderminster, a town in England's Midlands district. He began teaching himself guitar at age 14.

"I was in love with this girl," he confides in a soft, gentlemanly voice, "and I thought that if I could play guitar, maybe I could win her heart—and it certainly worked [*laughs*]. Hank Marvin & the Shadows were it for me—everybody I knew wanted to do that. I actually met Hank Marvin in Australia last year, and I said to him, 'If it hadn't been for you, I wouldn't be playing.' And Robert said, 'His mother hasn't forgiven you yet [*laughs*].' It was great."

Blunt's first gigs were at local clubs with a group called Butch Clutch & the Ex-cellerators. Robert Plant, who lived nearby, was fronting the Crawling Kingsnakes at the time, and, on occasion, he called on Robbie to fill in for his guitarist. Blunt made his recording debut in 1969, playing a Coral electric sitar on Gordon Jackson's *Thinking Back*, which also featured the members of Traffic.

"That electric sitar belonged to Steve Winwood, who's my idol," Blunt notes. "He's the best musician I've ever played with, or that I'm ever likely to play with or meet. He can play everything better than anybody."

In 1970, Robbie formed Bronco, a "flower-power" group that was influenced by the Buffalo Springfield, Country Joe & the Fish, and the Velvet Underground. He sang and played guitar on Bronco's *Country Home* and *Ace of Sunlight* albums. During his only U.S. tour with Bronco, he saw a musician who would change his course as a guitarist.

"I was of that school where it's what you don't play that makes it special."

"We'd been supporting Freddie King at the Whiskey in L.A., which was great, but seeing Duane Allman there with the Allman Brothers just blew me apart. I'd never seen anybody play slide. I went home and got all of his records and figured out his playing in an *E* open tuning. I learned every lick of his I could."

Robbie played slide extensively in his next groups, Silverhead and Broken Glass. With Silverhead, he recorded 1973's *Sixteen & Savaged*.

"That band was ahead of its time," he says, "almost like a punk sort of thing-a little glam, but pretty nasty. It carried some weight, too. Its singer, Michael Des Barre, just went on tour with the Power Station." Blunt appeared on *Broken Glass* in 1975 and then joined a regrouping of Chicken Shack for 1978's *The Creeper* and *That's the Way We Are*.

When Chicken Shack disbanded after its 1978 tour, Robbie returned to Kidderminster.

"I was probably at the lowest point in my life," he sighs. "I didn't have any money, I didn't have nothin'.'"

He came home again to Kidderminster about the same time that Led Zeppelin disbanded, and he began going over to Robert Plant's house to do some 4-track recording.

"I'd just sit in the studio and go direct with a Roland TR-808 drum machine," Robbie recalls. "The first day, I put this thing down which subsequently became 'Far Post'—it's on the B-side of Robert's 'Fat Lip' single. Robert heard it and said, 'That's great,' and in no time at all he had come up with some lyrics. We thought, let's do a show. Let's get this thing together."

Billing themselves as the Honeydrippers, they played a few club dates and began working on *Pictures at Eleven*. Keyboardist Jezz Woodroffe and bassist Paul Martinez were brought into the fold, and with Cozy Powell on drums, the Robert Plant band recorded its first cuts—"Like I've Never Been Gone" and "Slow Dancer"—at Rockfield Studios in Monmouth, England. Phil Collins played drums on the rest of the LP.

"It was great when we completed the first album," Robbie recalls. "It was like I'd been in the wilderness for years, trying to find my way out."

What do you enjoy most about playing with Robert Plant?

I suppose the challenge, really. I used to get paranoid about people comparing me to Jimmy Page. There again, I didn't join Led Zeppelin—I happen to play with Robert Plant. But it's almost like ever-present sometimes, yet it's a different kind of music, and I have a different approach.

Do you have to edit your playing? At times it sounds as if you consciously hold back.

Yeah, for sure. I was of that school where it's what you *don't* play that makes it special. On records, I usually show a certain amount of restraint and just pull it back a little notch or two. Whatever the record takes, you know—that's my job. I don't solo for the solo's sake. How would you describe your approach to soloing?

For starters, a solo should feel like it's part of the track and not just something stuck on like a postage stamp. I could probably play better if it were all live. There are certain things where it's almost like I'm penciling-in something to start with, and then I put the ink on. I really do think about a lot of those solos. I work them out, even. But then other times, I just go in and go for it. I'll stand in the control room and really get wound up. And everybody's winding me up, too. On the first album, there was a whole load of people having a party while I was trying to do my thing. But it did wind me up.

How much freedom do you have in the studio?

I can play pretty much what I want, although Robert tries to push me this way or whatever. I don't think he knows what he wants—I don't think any of us do. I mean, sometimes, I'll spend a couple of days figuring something out, and initially he won't like it, because he's thinking along something else. If I put a lot of time into something, I figure at the end of it, it's got to fit the tune. Usually he comes 'round and says, "yeah." On "Far Post," which hasn't appeared on any of the albums, I put on some harmony guitars. At the time, he said, "No, you can't do that—that's old hat." I said, "Okay, scrub 'em." I still had a mix of the track with the harmony guitars, and when we started the tour—this is like two-and-a-half years later—he said, "Do you still have a copy of 'Far Post'?" So when I played the mix, he said, "You know, those harmony guitars are great on there!" Doesn't that just say everything?

You feature a lot of different tones on record. Are you an equipment collector?

No. Anything that I buy, I utilize. I will not just buy guitars and stick them in a cupboard. I can't stand all that. You may as well go into the antique business! My favorite is a '56 Fender Strat with a '54 neck on it. I used mine on the first two albums. Actually, Robert said to me on the third album, "I don't want you to sound like that anymore," because he wanted to move it somewhere else. I can't believe it, but I never even used it on *Shaken 'N' Stirred.*

What song epitomizes that Strat's straight tone?

"Big Log," I suppose. That was just the old Strat through an old, pre-CBS Fender Princeton. The amp was one of the Who's, actually. I don't think there were any effects on that song. It's just got something—a beautiful tone.

What pickup configuration did you use for "Big Log"?

Basically, it was the treble pickup with the middle one. I have a five-position switch to have the facility to get the half-tone between the middle and treble pickup. It's the volume that seems to be more critical than anything. You can wind it around to 8 and just nudge it a little bit, and you get it just starting to break.

How do you approach cowriting songs with Robert Plant?

I usually come up with the guitar part, and then he constructs something over it. After that, we beat it into shape—bend it about a bit. But coming up with the basic idea is usually the norm. The only songs we wrote simultaneously were "In the Mood" and "Through with the Two-Step." For "In the Mood," it's my chord progression and solo—the middle part. I wanted to sound almost like the Beatles, you know. "Two Step" was the only one where Robert was so frustrated that he actually started singing something and we sat there trying to figure out what chords to pick behind it. For "Big Log," I wrote everything but the middle eight.

Does it feel like you've come a long way in the past few years?

Oh, yeah, I needed to. I was a desperate man. I'm happy with the way things are. As long as my output's good, I'm okay. If my output's not good, I have to do something about it. With the last album, my stock was depleted, but right now I'm starting to get a lot of ideas again, which is great. Maybe playing onstage again is inspiring me, or maybe I'm in love [*laughs*]. *—Excerpted from the October 1985 issue of* Guitar Player

Tommy Bolin

BY LOWELL CAUFFIEL | MARCH 1977

ALMOST AS DISTURBING AS TOMMY BOLIN'S DEATH ITSELF
(on December 4, 1976) was the fact that the 25-year-old musician's fatal drug over-
dose occurred just when he was emerging as a noted guitarist in progressive rock
and jazz-rock circles.

After being summoned to fill the shoes of first Joe Walsh in James Gang and later
Ritchie Blackmore in Deep Purple, Bolin could have easily been saddled with the
title of "best replacement guitarist." But Tommy's less publicized musical history
reveals a journeyman musician whose versatility was matched by a restlessness to
work and learn, the end result crystallizing into Bolin's own electric guitar style.

Born in Sioux City, Iowa, Bolin dropped out of high school at 16 and migrated
to Denver where he formed a band called Zephyr in 1968. After serving a blues ap-
prenticeship on the road with Albert King for a year, he made his way to New York
and its budding jazzrock scene in 1973. His reputation had expanded to the point
where Billy Cobham picked him for the session work on *Spectrum*, the drummer's
noted solo debut that Jeff Beck often credits as a major influence in sparking his jazz
pursuits.

Months later, Joe Walsh recommended Tommy for the lead slot in James Gang.
He appeared on two of the group's albums in the one year he was with the band. In
mid-summer of 1975, Bolin replaced Blackmore in Deep Purple, cowriting seven
of the tunes on *Come Taste the Band*. Perhaps realizing that in his work with these

two bands, coupled with a solo effort (*Teaser*), he'd written 33 songs in four albums, Bolin signed with Columbia to pursue his own career.

He had been touring with his own band following the release of his LP, *Private Eyes*, when he was found dead in a Miami hotel room. The following interview was conducted on October 7, just two months before his death.

What sparked your interest in music?

I was five or six at the time, I think, and I used to watch this show on TV called *Caravan of Stars*. I saw Elvis, Johnny Cash, Carl Perkins. After seeing them perform, I knew that was what I wanted to do.

What made you gravitate towards the guitar?

I actually started on drums when I was 13 and played them for two years. Then I went to guitar for a year, played keyboards for a year and a half, and went back to guitar. It was just the right instrument. You're in direct contact with the music you're making by having the strings under your fingers. It's not mechanical like a piano. My first guitar was a used Silvertone—the one that had the amplifier in the case. When I bought it, I had a choice between it or this black Les Paul for $75. I took the Silvertone. That was my first mistake.

Were there any particular guitarists who influenced you in your early days?

Well, Django Reinhardt and Carl Perkins. But, really, anything I heard I was influenced by. There wasn't any particular person, outside of Hendrix. In high school bands we used to play anything and everything—"96 Tears," "Gloria," "Hang On Sloopy," whatever. I used to listen a lot to Rolling Stones records and play along with them when I was first starting. I'd just experiment around the I-IV-V progression. It's a good way to learn—jamming around basic music—and the Rolling Stones' first album was pretty basic.

Did playing drums help your guitar work at all?

Definitely. Even now, I'll play drums a lot at home, and it will help my wrist action [for the picking hand] and keep certain things in line—like not speeding up or slowing down. I think the way I play the guitar is very percussive. I play a lot of rhythm chops as though I were playing congas or something.

What did you learn in playing behind Albert King?

I learned a lot about lead guitar—that you don't have to blow your cookies in the first bar. At that time, I was playing everything I knew when I took a lead. And he said, "Man, just say it all with one note." He taught me that it was much harder to be simple than to be complicated during solos. If you blow your cookies in the first bar, you have nowhere to go. Blues is really good that way. It teaches you to develop coherent solos, because the form you're playing over is so basic. You have to develop leads that go someplace. The neatest compliment I ever got was when I was play-

ing with Albert King at an indoor concert in Boulder, Colorado. He used to let me take solos, and I was very into playing that day. After the concert, he came up to me and said, "You got me today, but I'll get you tomorrow." I really respect him. He's a beautiful player.

Why all the interest in so many styles, and how did you handle them all?

They were just gigs that came up. I'd rather work than not. I was very lucky to be able to play in all those extremes. It was difficult following a guy like Ritchie Blackmore. When someone is the focal point of a group like he was, it's very hard to replace them. After a while, it just got to be pointless. The way I got involved in jazz-rock was through a flute player named Jeremy Steig. He showed me various jazz relationships and put them into a rock perspective, and then, through him, I met a lot of New York people like Billy Cobham and Jan Hammer.

Cobham called me for the *Spectrum* session, and I said, "I don't know how to read, man." He said it was okay. So I went to the studio, and he handed me a chart. I told him again I didn't know how to read, so we had a day of rehearsal and then cut the album in two days. In rehearsal, I'd just find out the changes—for example, Am to D9 to G6 to El3—and play around those chords and changes. I learned quite a bit through those people. You can't help but learn. All the different styles I've played have really helped me as a guitarist, and helped me develop my own way of playing. I have my own style, but it's different for each kind of music.

"I saw Elvis, Johnny Cash, Carl Perkins. After seeing them perform, I knew that was what I wanted to do."

What about your equipment?

I'm using two Hiwatt tops with four Sound City bottoms. The Stratocaster I use is a stock 1963. It's very hot, and I really don't know why. I use Ernie Ball Extra Super Slinky strings for the Strat because my hands aren't very strong. I use heavy picks, Herco gold, but I chew them all day first. It loosens them up and gives them a feeling somewhere between a heavy and medium thickness.

Do you prefer the highs of a Fender to the thicker Gibson sound?

Yes, I like the cutting sound of a Fender. With Les Pauls, at least for me, I can get only two or three different tones. That's it. But with the Strat, I can use it on about everything I play. I keep the amp on full bass with no treble, and I also use a Sam Ash fuzz tone. You can't get those anymore. I have the fuzz on all the time with Attack, Volume, and Tone all the way up. It doesn't sound like a fuzz, really. It just gives the guitar so much more bite and attack.

How do you get such a smooth tone with the fuzz on all the time?

Having the bass up on the amp is the ticket. Plus you have to work a lot with the tone controls on the guitar. You have to use a lot of bass because the Strat has such a thin sound. The tone I have now is somewhere between a Strat and a Les Paul.

One of your characteristics as a guitarist seems to be triplets. Do you hammer yours or pick each one?

I probably play them too much. I pick each one. I think the ability to do that, again, comes from the drums. The drums strengthened my wrist, which allows me to keep my picking hand relaxed when I play. That's important, and it comes from doing it for a long time. How good you play triplets—or anything really—comes from the way you attack the notes. You have to attack with confidence. Practice gives you that, I guess. For me, practice isn't doing scales, but doing things like writing, jamming with other people, or playing gigs.

Looking back, would you have done anything differently?

A lot of times I wish I would have learned to read. But I'm very impatient. I used to try and take things in leaps and bounds. Now I've realized it's got to be step by step. —*Excerpted from the March 1977 issue of* Guitar Player

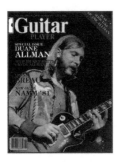

Lenny Breau

BY BRAWNER SMOOT | OCTOBER 1981

"LENNY IS THE GREATEST GUITAR PLAYER IN THE WORLD

today. I think he knows more guitar than any guy that has ever walked the face of the earth, because he can play jazz, he can play a little classical, he can play great country, and he does it all with taste."

This profound plaudit, exclaimed by no less than guitar genius Chet Atkins in the. October '79 issue of *Frets*, may seem hyperbolic—that is, until you've heard Lenny Breau play.

Lenny Breau was born in Auburn, Maine, on August 5, 1941, to country music performers Hal Lone Pine and Betty Cote. The family soon moved to Canada, and by age eight, Lenny began playing the guitar.

"My folks were on the road doing a country and western thing, sort of like the Grand Ole Opry," Breau explains. "In fact, they even did a few tours with the Opry. Anyway, there always were a lot of guitars around—that's all you saw in country bands during those days. I used to eye the lead player, Ray Couture, who was in my father's band. He was my first teacher.

"I'd watch the country stuff he was doing—some of the more commercial things like boogie woogies—but he also listened to Django Reinhardt, and he had old 78s he'd play in his room. But I didn't appreciate Django then, because I didn't really know what jazz was. I was still learning my basic chords."

Breau's chord practice during this time was done on Gene Autry and Roy Rogers guitars sold by Sears. Three years later, Lenny got a flat-top Gibson, and he discovered the fascinating rhythms of Chet Atkins on the radio.

"I heard him play, and I said, 'Gee, he has got to be doing something more than strumming.' Where I lived on the farm, everyone was more or less strumming everything. Once in a while, you heard some singlestring, but you never heard fingerstyle like Chet's. So, I immediately tried to imitate him, but it was pretty hard to do without anyone showing you how."

When Breau was 14 he moved to Schenectady, New York, where he began scrutinizing jazz recordings. Tal Farlow, Johnny Smith, and Barney Kessel became major influences, and Chet Atkins still held a strong place in the young musician's growing repertoire. Eventually, his reputation grew so quickly in Canada that he hosted his own TV show out of Winnipeg for the Canadian Broadcasting Company. Breau also did a lot of studio recording in Canada—everything from pop and jazz to rock and roll. He was also employed as a staff guitarist for local TV and radio stations.

Eventually, Lenny Breau became famous for being able to walk bass lines while simultaneously comping chords and adding a melody line on top. He sometimes sounded like three guitars.

"I think in terms of the colors and inversions of the chords."

Let's talk a little about your equipment—especially your Tom Holmes guitar.

I had that made in Nashville about two years ago, the idea being I enjoyed playing classical guitars. I like the way they feel, and I always practice on one, so I said to myself, "Well, why not have an electric guitar made with an extra-wide neck so that when I go from one instrument to another there's no change. It feels like you're playing classical all the time." So, that's why I had the Holmes made that way, and I had its neck fashioned a little longer to get more sustain and to give me more playing room. Once I'm past the 12th fret, if I'm playing high up on the neck, I want the frets to be a little bit farther apart than they are usually.

Is that because you want more room for chording?

Exactly. If you try to play a six-note chord up there, usually there isn't enough room. But on the Holmes there is.

Which string gauges are you most comfortable with on the Holmes?

I'm currently using .010, .012, a wound .018 G, .022, .032, and .042. I sometimes use an unwound G on studio things to, you know, get that sound, but they don't stay in tune good enough for me and unwounds tend to be a bit too loud. I want the E, A, D, and G strings to have a sound apart from the B and high E—which they don't when I use an unwound G. I want my chords to sound warm, so I use the wound string.

When fingerpicking, do you use nail only or a combination of nail and flesh?

I use mostly nails—unless they're too short. Then the skin will be there, too. But the sound I'm after is all nails, so I grow them a little longer than usual. You see, instead of picking straight across the strings, I pick sideways a lot of the time—especially on slow tunes like ballads.

It's a very delicate touch.

It's like rubbing the note, and I key my Fender Twin for a real soft sound, too. My playing's sort of like playing on a piano with the soft pedal while the sustain pedal is always down.

Do you shape your nails?

Yeah, I have to be pretty careful with them. I read where Chet Atkins said he wears gloves sometimes when he takes a shower. It's funny, but probably true because his nails are on the thin side, and when you get nails wet they're a lot easier to break.

From whom did you get your slurring techniques?

From listening to flamenco players like Sabicas and Montoya.

When you improvise, do you think in terms of tonal colors or scales?

I think in terms of the colors and inversions of the chords. When I play chords, I consider the inversions, because every inversion has its own color. If one color is blue, another may also be blue—but a different shade. Every time you play a different inversion that shade will change. That's why I think of painting with the guitar, because when you mix colors you get different shades. I also play from modes and scales. If I'm doing a tune I always keep in mind the melody, or the essence of it—unless I'm doing something freer where I'm more on emotions and going from chord to chord without having a definite structure.

One technique that has become somewhat of a trademark of yours is octave harmonics. When did you first incorporate them into your style, and do you recall how you first used them?

I first heard Chet Atkins do them. He'd pick both the note and the harmonic together. That was the first technique I learned, but I changed it a little. I played the note first, then the harmonic.

If you play an arpeggiated harmonic on a six-note chord, do you usually strike a note first before hitting the harmonic?

Right. Say it's a six-string chord like an *Am9*. You start on the fourth string, and play the *G* note—so that would be a straight note—then you play a harmonic on the *A* note on the sixth string. Do that all the way up. On the way down, it's just the opposite—harmonic then note.

You have a technique where you pick a flurry of notes while almost totally muting the strings, giving a very percussive sound. How long have you been doing that?

Quite a long time. It came from playing those Sabicas pull-offs and the Montoya stuff and muffling it. Muting gives a percussive effect, and by getting a good strong pulloff it almost sounds like all the notes are picked. There's yet another illusion. It's hard to tell which notes are picked and which aren't, because the idea is to get the pull-offs as loud as the notes. Here, like when playing octave harmonics, you have to pick the note a little softer and get the pull-off a little stronger to create the illusion of balance.

How do you feel when you see talented and artistically sincere musicians going unrecognized because of the way the music industry functions?

It's depressing. It makes you feel bad. Of course, it's probably better in this country than in a lot of other ones. In some countries, you're not allowed to express yourself at all unless you play ball with whoever's running things. In Russia, I'm sure the musicians feel a little bit held back. It's not that bad here, but I'd like to see more airplay given to artistic stuff, and it's not happening. You really have to look for it.

Has that ever been difficult for you in terms of choosing your own path of going for art, as opposed to dollars?

Has it been hard for me choosing my own path? Well, not too hard, because money never meant that much to me. I mean it did, but not to the point where I wouldn't play something. I just made a commitment to the music, and I was hoping there would be real good money in it. Well, like maybe there will be someday, but it's just like painting. You've got to paint what you want to paint, whether it's selling or not, and if you want to make money, then you paint what's going to sell. When you realize how short life is, anyway, what good is money? You can get all that money, but you aren't going to live that long to spend it. For me, it's much more enjoyable to play what you want to play, regardless of the situation. The self-satisfaction—that's what I've always felt. So I didn't have any problem in picking a path. Of course, there are hard times—like how am I going to pay the rent this month, or something like that. But I wouldn't have it any other way. —*Excerpted from the October 1981 issue of* Guitar Player

Jon Brion

BY MICHAEL MOLENDA | FEBRUARY 2005

FEW MUSICAL MOMENTS PRODUCE BIGGER GOOSEBUMPS
than the psychic power flush that occurs when something unique and revolutionary
slams into your eardrums. You know the feeling—it engulfed you the first time you
heard Jimi Hendrix or Jeff Beck or Kurt Cobain or whomever your personal totem
might have been—and the epiphany kicked you right in the ass, because it proved
that fresh possibilities existed in something you had accepted as comfortably inert.
("There's nothing new in music" being the battle cry of unbelievers, lazy thinkers,
and those who fear change.)

Although not, by strict definition, a guitar *hero*, multi-instrumentalist Jon Brion is
also one of those unfettered, immensely gifted artists who challenges creative stasis
and discovers new turns in roads seemingly well traveled. His work with Aimee
Mann, David Byrne, Fiona Apple, Rufus Wainwright, and others—as well as his
brilliant 2001 solo album *Meaningless*, his contributions to the *Magnolia* soundtrack,
and his recent score for *I Heart Huckabees*—renders somewhat conventional songcraft strange and newly exciting. Using complex guitar and keyboard textures,
startling tonal choices, beautifully fractured melodicism, and poignant harmonic
excursions, Brion's applied intellectualism destroys convention while simultaneously seducing listeners through their base pleasure receptors. Like the angel who
falls to earth in Wim Wenders' *Wings of Desire*, Brion is both ethereal and sensually
grounded. Study him and be changed.

How do you craft such idiosyncratic guitar parts and textures?

Modern or unique sounds are simply combinations of preexisting things. One of my epiphanies was discovering a lot of techniques used by country players were not being employed by rock guitarists. Internal string bending—where one of your fingers is bending a note *within* a chord—is a very common technique if you're a country or country-rock player wielding a Telecaster with a clean sound, but you don't hear it much elsewhere. I realized that I could integrate that technique with other styles of guitar playing I liked. Then I added distortion, which was incredible because it lets you control the rate at which the harmonics beat against each other by varying how much you bend one string in and out of tune. You can create some pretty avant-garde sounds that way. But these embellishments should always be fluid and mysterious. I don't want a listener to sit down and say, "Oh, that's interesting. Bar one is Roger McGuinn meets Fred Frith, and bar two is country twang meets Metallica." That would ruin it for me. I'm way more delighted when someone hears a little guitar blip or a bizarre chord that makes them want to go back and listen to a song multiple times.

It's amazing that you often construct these remarkable soundscapes without effects, plug-ins, or digital-audio manipulations. It's mostly done organically between you, a guitar, and an amp.

There are so many techniques that put the power in *your* hands—which, to me, is always a good thing. The more your hands can be the important part of the tonal equation, the more your playing will highlight your particular style of expression. If you string up eight effects in a row, it's near impossible to hear the personality of the player anymore. In fact, it almost doesn't matter who the player is, because all the compression and delays and reverbs and multiple distortion boxes make the whole sound totally generic. I don't want my sound neutered by some chorus pedal that destroys personality—I want people to hear every little pop and click of the strings when I have my fingers on the instrument. So I'd rather construct tones with a weird amp and guitar combination—some tiny '50s practice amp that's on the verge of dying, and a guitar that makes a "gwonk" sound because it only has three really dead strings left on it.

I was also greatly influenced by seeing Les Paul perform live, because he uses every part of the guitar to generate tone. In the course of one line, he might play very close to the bridge on the lowest string with the treble pickup selected and the tone full up. Then, a few notes later, he'll play the same line four octaves up on the E string with the neck pickup selected and the tone knob turned all the way down. It's so brilliant! First, you hear this really low melody that's extremely thin and bright, and then you hear this incredibly high line that's really, really dark. The level of expression you can get from that approach is just extraordinary.

But it's not just sound that makes your playing unique—there's also a cross-pollination of stylistic elements that makes for an unusual *musical* blend.

Juxtaposition is what makes creative things interesting. I like pitting one element against another or taking something that would not normally appear in rock music and drag it into a three-minute pop song. So if you want to sound different, go out and buy a bunch of records that have nothing to do with the type of music you're playing—even if you hate it. If you play heavy metal, for example, go get something really wussy. I guarantee that if you really listen, you'll find something that interests you, and you'll probably absorb that new element into your style. You see, nothing comes from Mars, and everything is here to be discovered if you look in the right places. Take the Beatles, for example. When they were hanging out with the London art crowd and discovering John Cage and Indian music and all this stuff, they brought those influences back to the studio.

"Juxtaposition is what makes creative things interesting."

Now, back then, people thought they had carried some kind of new music out of the ether. But the truth was that they were simply being inquisitive about music *outside* of their own. Unfortunately, I don't see today's bands doing this type of exercise to the extent they should.

Why not?

Well, let's face it, most people are sheep, and that's problem number one—it's safer to follow than to lead. Problem number two is that it's natural for musicians to emulate the things they like to hear. I'm as guilty of this as anyone else. If you grew up thinking Ace Frehley was the greatest guitarist in the world, then chances are you're still playing that second-generation Chuck Berry stuff. I don't think it's necessarily bad to have major influences, but it gets ugly if you only listen to one thing and try to emulate it as closely as possible. To me, someone who just nails Hendrix is fairly boring, whereas someone who *absorbs* Hendrix but who does his own thing is pretty cool.

It also doesn't seem as if diversity is as highly valued and sought after as it may have been in the Beatles' heyday.

True. These days, someone who is beholden to jangly rock—and who thinks all soloing is bad and all noise stuff is just wanking—is not going to be open to the influence of some very exciting and progressive guitar players.

Such as?

Fred Frith is an unbelievable genius of the instrument. That more people don't throw rose petals in front of him when he walks is an absolute mystery to me. And if we're talking about people who should have rose petals thrown in front of them, you must include Ry Cooder. He is consistently in touch with the quest for tone, and he really works to ensure that what the listener hears is as close to the intention of the music as possible. I think he's constantly dissatisfied because he's on a very tough quest, but for the rest of us, hearing his fingers moving across the strings to generate deep and heartfelt tones is just gorgeous. Then there's somebody like Jerry Donohue, who has invented entirely new techniques for playing guitar—even if the only people who use them are country players. Robert Fripp is amazing, as well.

What's your main beef with some of today's players?

It's that most rock guitarists simply don't *rock*. They might nod their heads to the rhythm, but their sound is like a paper wall. They use such light strings that if you hit one hard, it goes sharp, so they all develop this very delicate right-hand technique. Well, sorry, but rock guitar is all about attack. It's a sound that, to me, is defined by Pete Townshend's awesome power chords. I wish more younger guitarists would relate to him and players such as Stevie Ray Vaughan and Jeff Beck. Stevie used very thick strings, and his right hand was incredibly muscular, and that's part of what gave his sound its visceral punch. If you listen to Jeff Beck's Yardbirds stuff, you'll hear a guy with phenomenal attack in his right hand fighting with all his will to make something cool out of the basic equipment available to him at the time.

Are there any modern guitarists who you view as standouts?

Tom Morello is *the* great modern rock guitarist. The way most people have made crazy influential music for centuries is that they grab something from a type of music their audience *isn't* listening to. Morello was influenced by DJs, and he figured out how to scratch using a guitar. The first time I heard that, I practically drove off the road. It was one of those moments where you hear something and you can't even believe it exists. It was such a simple idea, but it was beautifully executed, and it rocked. The instant I heard him, I thought, "That's it. He beat everybody. He's the best guy on the planet now."

At this point, I should ask what your gear main setup is before we forget about the tools of the trade entirely.

My main live guitar is this ancient Les Paul carcass that has been stripped of all its originality. It's a '52 body that had been refinished at some point, and its pickups taken out at another. I think somebody tried to make it look like a late-'50s Les Paul to resell it, without realizing they had one of the earliest ones ever made! I also have a '54 Gretsch Duo Jet that has been a constant companion over the years, as well as a Hofner guitar shaped like a Beatle Bass, which happens to be the finest sounding guitar I own. Those are the main things in the arsenal, and then I have all this bizarre stuff that isn't very interesting to read about, such as no-name guitars that make one incredible kind of sound but that aren't very versatile. I also have tons of strange, unidentified amplifiers from '60s companies that never took off.

Okay, what do you think it will take to get musicians to stop settling for the status quo?

It doesn't help that "intellectual" is such a dirty word these days. People think if somebody uses their intellect they're going to make cold music—well, screw that! Here, as we discuss the act of making music, it's an intellectual thing. But at the point where I put the instrument in my hands, my conscious mind goes to whatever the music place is, and I'm gone. Then, at the moment I put down the guitar in-between takes, I'm back into the intellectual approach, assessing whether what I'm doing sounds too normal or clichéd or whatever. And when the tape starts rolling again, I'm off the ground once more. It's a cycle of intellect and pure feeling. I think the *lack* of intellect in music is what should be feared most. It's shameful that so many guitarists copy whatever is popular when it's so easy to seek out uninhabited areas. There are so many variables to explore between your consciousness, your hands, your interests, your tone, getting things on tape, how your part relates to the other aspects of the arrangement, and how the finished record relates to other things around the world. It's infinite. But even considering all of the intellectual options of music making, I can still pick up a guitar, play a simple D chord, and just smile.

Michael Brook

BY JAMES ROTONDI | JUNE 1998

MICHAEL BROOK IS ORIGINALLY FROM TORONTO, BUT THE
guitarist sounds strangely at home playing on records by Indian mandolin virtuoso
U. Srinivas, and the late Pakistani singer Nusrat Fateh Ali Khan—just two of the
global artists he has produced for Peter Gabriel's Real World label. Although Brook
has made frequent trips to India and studied Eastern music in the '70s with Jon
Hassell and Pandit Pran Nath, his immersion in that culture does not fully explain
his natural touch in translating Hindustani music into ambient funk. The easy stylistic coexistence is less due to intense study than it is to Brook's musical instincts,
common sense, and uncommonly wellhoned set of ears.

"In some ways, naivete is a huge aid," he says. "You're not aware of all the things
you're doing wrong. I listen to the music of the artists and cultures I work with, but
I don't necessarily have a technical mastery of the styles. I just try to make the music
sound good, and I think a lot of the musicians from other cultures that I work with
feel that way, too. They know exactly what they're doing in their own musical language, but when some kind of hybrid occurs, they're *all* playing it by ear."

Fittingly, it was Brook's 1985 solo record, *Hybrid*, produced and performed with
Brian Eno and Daniel Lanois, that not only set his course as a global music explorer,
but introduced his distinctive "infinite guitar" technique. The characteristic sustain
of Brook's infinite guitar (similar to the sound of an EBow) is produced by circuitry
that sends the signal from one pickup into another, causing a feedback loop. Brook

merely holds a finger down on the neck to produce a sustained tone. The design is approximated by the Fernandes Sustainer, but the guitarist/producer is keeping mum about the actual details.

"I get no benefit from sharing it," he shrugs. "As it is, if someone needs infinite guitar, I get the call."

Although the performance of infinite guitar requires a technical device, the style is a product of more philosophical leanings.

"The sustained, ornamented quality of the infinite guitar is based on an Eastern aesthetic," says Brook. "The sound bears some resemblance to an instrument called a *shenai*—a doublereed, midrange-toned instrument popularized by a musician who has been very influential on my playing, Bismallah Khan."

The attributes of infinite guitar—rapid slurs, horn-like overtones, half-step ghost notes—are aided by Brook's use of an Electro-Harmonix Deluxe Memory Man analog delay. At the end of a note, for example, Brook often sweeps the delay time control with his foot, causing a sudden gurgling pitch bend.

"In some ways, naivete is a huge aid."

Although Brook sports a Fender Deluxe Reverb and a Sears Airline guitar on his recent bluesy soundtrack for the film *Albino Alligator*, he rarely brings an amp into the studio. Typically, he opts for a complex effects chain run direct into the recording console. The signal from his '80s Tokai Strat first hits a Hot Tubes fuzzbox ("used purely as a buffer, so I can run the guitar through a lot of pedals and get less noise"). From there, the signal flows to a DOD compressor, a Yamaha 6-band graphic EQ, a Korg Overdrive, a SansAmp PSA-I, the Deluxe Memory Man, and a BSS Direct Box.

To warm up the tone, the effects chain is routed into a modified Neve 1073 preamp, a Drawmer M -500 compressor, and, finally, the mixer. Brook also exploits the echo and "resonant chord" features of an Eventide H3000 Ultra Harmonizer, and calls on an Electro-Harmonix 16-second Digital Delay for loops and backwards guitar. And while he usually shuns amplification, Brook often positions mics in front of the studio monitors as he plays and mixes in the "live" tracks to taste during the mix.

Carrie Brownstein and Corin Tucker

BY DARRIN FOX | DECEMBER 2003

OVER THE COURSE OF EIGHT YEARS, SLEATER-KINNEY HAVE
thrived in the indie-rock movement. The bass-less trio from Olympia, Washington,
has built a loyal fan base, released a steady stream of critically lauded albums, and
has produced tighter tunes and broader tonal colors with each subsequent record.
Along the way, they've taken nary a misstep—a Herculean task in a music biz that
has little patience for the phrase "artist development." Helping drive the band's
ascension into indie bliss are Corin Tucker and Carrie Brownstein, whose agitated
guitar stylings rub against each other with just enough friction to give the group's
pop tendencies a righteous middle finger.

Do the two of you have designated roles?

Brownstein: Corin definitely plays more of the bass lines—even though it's a guitar—and I typically do the leads.

Were the roles blurred before?

Brownstein: They weren't necessarily blurred, but by the third or fourth record,
we were realizing what worked, and that meant using Corin's guitar more and more
to fill in the low end. Once you start relying on something sonically, it kind of ties
you into a certain kind of style.

Tucker: To get that low end, I plug my Danelectro DC-3 into an A/B box, which goes to two amps: a Music Man combo and a Fender Dual Showman running through an Ampeg 4x12 cabinet. Onstage, I put the Music Man behind me and the Dual Showman is behind Carrie. My effects are a Vox overdrive and a Boss EQ pedal.

Brownstein: My main guitar is a '72 Gibson SG. I'm really comfortable with the neck, and I perform the best on that guitar in the studio. So when I want a different tone, it's usually a matter of changing the amp around or plugging in a different pedal. Sometimes, we'll crank up a Fender Champ or an old Ampeg for natural amp distortion. I'll also use my main stage amp—a Vox AC30. For effects, I use a Boss Blues Driver, a Line 6 ML4 modulation pedal, and a Dunlop CryBaby.

"When we write, it's all about the parts. The sonic character comes in later."

Was the decision not to have a bass player in the band a calculated one?

Brownstein: No. Neither Corin nor I play bass, nor do we want to play bass. We've always liked the dynamics and chemistry between three people onstage, but not having a bassist challenged us to come up with a unique kind of music, as well as a different style as guitar players.

Tucker: I also think there's a frenetic energy with just our two guitars that we like, and we didn't want to risk losing that by adding another instrument to the mix.

How do you approach writing your riffs?

Brownstein: No matter what type of music I'm listening to, what always catches me before the vocal comes in is when the band is playing a good riff. That's what appeals to me about early blues stuff like Muddy Waters or Robert Johnson—or even mid-period blues like Buddy Guy or B. B. King. Before they start singing, the band is chugging on a riff. So, when I'm writing, I always think, "If I can just come up with a good riff everything else will fall into place." If the riff isn't interesting, it's hard for me to stay engaged as a listener. And when I play live, it's fun to have a cool riff that starts the song. When we write, it's all about the parts. The sonic character comes in later.

During the writing process, does Corin come in with chord progression, and then you lay a riff over that?

Brownstein: Actually it's sort of reversed. I often come in with a riff, and Corin will fill out the chord progression underneath it. It's almost like the song is written inside out.

Is there a particular two-guitar band that has had a big influence on you guys?

Brownstein: I would say Television. Richard Lloyd and Tom Verlaine had an amazing language that they spoke with their guitars.

Carrie Brownstein (left) and Corin Tucker (right).

Tucker: Definitely Sonic Youth. Beat Happening was another two-guitar and drum band that was a big influence, as well.

Do you consider yourself perfectionists in the studio?

Brownstein: Only in the sense that I won't let anything stand if it makes me cringe. I think that one important lesson to learn is that some mistakes are good. I don't like listening to records that are too perfect. When I listen to a song, and I can hear the vocalist take a gasp, or hear a note in the solo that is kind of muted—like the guitarist didn't hit it quite perfectly—it's great. That's character.

But where do you draw the line between character and a bad performance?

Brownstein: The part in question shouldn't distract from the song. If I'm in the moment, for example, and there's something that's a little bit off, but it's a cool mistake that adds to the song, then we usually keep it.

Do you still get asked a lot of questions about what it's like to be in such a male-dominated industry?

Brownstein: Yeah. It was annoying, but now it has just become interesting. Fielding those questions has become part of the experience of playing music for me. A while back, I realized that no man has ever been asked how does it feel to be a man playing in a band. I'd like to think that music isn't gender specific.

Why is a woman playing guitar in a rock band still such a big deal?

Brownstein: Many of the rock icons are male, so I think it's hard for women to break through all that. In general, I think women are socialized to think that their role in music is relegated to singing or doing something that's kind of an appendage to the rest of the band. When you only see yourself represented in the media that way, then you have no way of understanding all the possibilities that are out there for you.

If there were more women guitarists, young girls would definitely see that as a viable option. I just don't think they're seeing that right now. It's "I can be Britney Spears and wear a half-shirt and dance around." Sure, that's easier—and you get more attention for it—but the more women who actually play guitar are seen, the more other women are going to know that it's something they can do, too.

Roy Clark

BY JON SIEVERT | NOVEMBER 1978

ENTERTAINER ROY CLARK IS PROBABLY THE MOST VISIBLE guitarist in America today. Nearly 35 million viewers tune in 52 weeks a year to see his pickin' and grinnin' on television's *Hee Haw*. Another 15 million or so see him on the nights when he hosts the *Tonight Show* and almost always sings and plays a song. Then, of course, there are the untold millions who catch him on his numerous TV guest spots on the afternoon talk shows or prime-time variety shows and specials. And last, but hardly least, are the several hundred thousand fans who see him live in concert during the 250 or so dates he does each year, crisscrossing the country and featuring his guitar out front in his multifaceted act. Not even the most widely acclaimed guitar legends can match this kind of exposure.

Of course, Roy Clark's high visibility can be attributed to other resources besides his guitar playing. He is an outstanding banjo picker and a masterful comic. And his fine singing voice has aided a very fertile 18-year recording career that has produced a long string of hit records on the country charts and several that have crossed over to the pop category. Roy's music industry awards would probably fill a room. In addition to the gold records, there are the results of his unprecedented sweep of the major country awards in 1974 when he was voted Entertainer of the Year by both the Country Music Association and the Academy of Country Music. Also during that same year, the American Guild of Variety Artists selected him Country Music Star of the Year.

Clark also holds an armful of awards attesting to his virtuosity on guitar, banjo, fiddle, and several other popular stringed instruments. Readers of *Music City News* have voted him Instrumentalist of the Year several times, as did the Country Association in 1977. *Playboy* readers have chosen him Picker of the Year twice. And since Chet Atkins ascended to *Guitar Player*'s Gallery of the Greats, Roy appears to have become heir apparent to *GP*'s Best Country Guitarist award in the annual readership poll.

Music came early to Roy Clark. Born to a musical family in Meaherrin, Virginia, on April 15, 1933, he made his public performing debut at

"I've really been influenced by everyone."

age four, singing "Last Night as I Lay on the Prairie." His mother was a pianist. His father, originally a tobacco farmer who moved to Washington, D.C., to accept a job when Roy was 11, often moonlighted five nights a week playing guitar, banjo, and fiddle. Roy began to beat around on a banjo and then a mandolin at a young age, but it wasn't until he was 14 that he fully tuned in to the sound of a neighbor's guitar and developed an overwhelming passion for playing. That year, for Christmas, he got his first guitar—a Sears Silvertone that cost $14.95. Within two weeks, he had mastered open chords and was playing behind his father at a square dance. From then on, his father made sure that Roy got around to see the wide variety of musicians playing in the Washington, D.C., area. The city was, and is, a veritable melting pot of people from all over the world that features nearly every kind of music. That appreciation of variety has always been evident in Roy's work and has allowed him to defy strict categorization.

Soon after his first intense learning burst on the guitar, Roy developed the same passion for the 5-string banjo—a passion he soon parlayed into two National Banjo Championships at ages 16 and 17. The second win carried an appearance at Nashville's Grand Ole Opry. Through his late teens and early twenties, he continued to hone his skills as an instrumentalist/vocalist/humorist, playing bars, dances, and on local TV and radio in the D.C. area. During this period, Roy seriously considered professional baseball, and, at 18, he actually turned professional boxer, winning 15 straight fights as a light-heavyweight before the 16th bout convinced him to try something else.

In about 1955, a local TV appearance led to a radio job with singer Jimmy Dean, who was then a kingpin on the local Washington scene but not yet the national star he would become. The two worked together on radio and TV, and when Dean left for New York, Roy took over the gig with his own special blend of instrumental flash pieces, singing, and humor. In 1960, with things going very smoothly, Roy decided it was time to make a career decision. Though his job was quite comfortable, he began looking for a way out of town. Along came country singer Wanda Jackson, on her way to the Las Vegas Golden Nugget club and looking for a guitar player and frontman for her band. Roy fit the bill.

Clark stayed with Jackson for a little over a year—long enough play lead guitar on her biggest hit, "Let's Have a Party." It was also Roy's good fortune that Jackson's manager was a showbizsavvy man named Jim Halsey, who had previously managed singer/guitarist Hank Thompson. Halsey quickly recognized the superstar potential of Roy's collective talents. When Jackson dissolved her band, Halsey became Roy's first and, to date, only manager. The two quickly negotiated a recording contract, and Roy's first album, *The Lightning Fingers of Roy Clark*, was soon released by Capitol Records.

At the same time, Roy began to intensify his television work. He had always been aware of the potential of the medium, having appeared on it for the first time in 1948, when he sang on *The Hayloft Conservatory of Musical Interpretation* show. He had appeared on local variety shows, but his manager began to place him in different settings, such as the dual-comedy role of Cousin Roy and (in drag) Big Mama Halsey on one of the most popular shows in the country, *The Beverly Hillbillies*. His biggest national breakthrough, however, came in January 1963, when he was selected as a guest for the Tonight Show during the interim period after Jack Paar left and before Johnny Carson took over. His old friend and partner Jimmy Dean was the guest host who chose him to appear. His successful guest spot eventually led to his first invitation to host the show himself.

Subsequently, Roy has turned up on just about every variety and celebrity show in existence, including the *Mike Douglas, Merv Griffin, Dinah Shore, Flip Wilson,* and *Hollywood Squares* programs. Guest acting roles included appearances on *The Odd Couple* and *Love, American Style*. And though television was providing widespread exposure, Roy did not neglect his live concerts—hitting the road at a rate of 250 shows a year, thereby providing direct personal contact with his fans.

In 1969, CBS came to him with a pilot for a cornball, countrystyle version of *Laugh-In* and asked him to cohost it with singer Buck Owens. Though dubious at first, Roy took the challenge, and *Hee Haw* very quickly jumped to the top of the summer ratings and won a regular spot in the fall lineup of shows. In 1971, with ratings still very high, CBS decided to cancel the show. Almost immediately it was put into syndication and has since become one of the most popular syndicated shows in history. Since then, Roy's popularity has continued to mushroom with guest spots, commercials, concerts, and a recording career that spans nearly 40 albums. He has a nearly unique ability to completely erase the distinctions between country and pop—a talent that has allowed him to establish some landmarks for country performers. He was one of the first to headline his own show in the big showrooms along the Las Vegas hotel strip and is certainly the most popular country musician in that town today. He currently plays the Frontier for two shows a day, seven nights a week, 12 weeks a year, to sellout crowds.

He was the first country artist to headline his own show in the Soviet Union, playing to enthusiastic, turn-away crowds in a 21-day, three-city tour in January 1976. He is also the first country performer to appear in the famous Movieland Wax Museum in Buena Park, California.

These days, Roy continues the workaholic schedule he has always maintained—though now that means his life is planned almost to the hour as much as six months in advance, and his schedule is handed to him on a computer printout. To meet this backbreaking cycle of concerts, television, recording, commercials, and, most recently, movies, Roy pilots his Mitsubishi MU- 2J turboprop plane in and out of the airports of America en route to his jobs.

This interview was conducted in Las Vegas, where Roy was playing the Desert Inn for the first time. Not surprisingly, Roy's audience looked pretty much like the same crowd he drew several weeks later in San Carlos, California—a cross section of the down-home side of America that is really a reflection of the man himself. Though he is probably the highest-paid performer in country music, Roy maintains a strong one-to-one relationship with his audience of devoted fans, signing autographs and establishing a personal contact with each person he meets.

You're known as a multitalented entertainer. How much of you is Roy Clark the guitarist?

Well, I think that is what I am, basically a guitar player—although I get frustrated because I don't play enough. I see a kid playing six hours a night in a club, and he's got fantastic chops, and I look at him and think, "Where did it go? I used to be able to do that!" I could play that way all night long, and even faster than I could think at one time. Now, I'm doing two shows a night, seven nights a week, and I am playing probably only 7 minutes per show—say, 15 total minutes a night. Although I'm onstage quite a bit, that's the actual playing. So how in the world are you going to keep your chops that way?

Does your schedule ever leave time for practice?

I do what I can. I keep a classical guitar at the house, and I practice on it a little, but that doesn't really take the place of concentrated practice on new things. It's important to make sure you are working on different licks so you don't get locked into the same old ones. You may really be able to do them great, but when a chance comes for a little challenge, you are not coordinated enough to do it. You may be able to hear it but not get it out the ends of your fingers. You end up just about a bar behind everything you're trying to play.

What was your first good guitar?

I got a used Martin D-18 around 1948. My dad traded an old shotgun, a fishing pole, a banjo head, and about 20 bucks for it.

When did you take up the banjo intensely?

I guess around age 15. When I started playing guitar, I became really aware of all the different sounds and things going on. That was about the time that [bluegrass banjo legend] Earl Scruggs was really hot. We used to listen to him on the Grand Ole Opry radio show on Saturday nights, and I would visualize him as having 14 fingers. There was no way you could figure out how he was getting all this pickin' out of one instrument. All the banjo players I had ever seen played with the Grandpa Jones frailin' style. So I traded an old Gibson F-4 mandolin I had for an old Washburn 5-string without a resonator, and I started pickin' at it. I got a lot of help from a cousin of Earl's named Smitty Irvin and a friend named Buster Austin. They really got me started, so I began using the banjo and the guitar. Then I bought another mandolin and a fiddle and started playing them, too. I would just buy an instrument, go and find somebody who played it, and just bug him until he showed me something on it.

When did you go electric?

The first thing I did was put a DeArmond pickup on that Martin, and that really blew my mind. I got into picking, and the guys I was playing with couldn't hold me back. I just wanted to pick, and they said, "Hey, you're supposed to be playing rhythm." And I'd say, "Yeah, but let me get out here in the front and grin a lot." Eventually, my dad bought me a King Recorder. That was my first real electric guitar. Later on, I had an S.S. Stewart archtop with a DeArmond pickup on it. That was one of the prettiest guitars I'd ever seen. It was blond with a checkerboard trim around it.

I will never forget the first night a guy came into a club I was playing and brought a Fender. I think it was one of the first Telecasters that came out, and I thought, "What is this world coming to?" That thing sounded so clean, and it really cut through for lead work. It just seemed unreal. In 1951, I won a banjo contest down in Warrenton, Virginia, and I used the prize money to buy my first Fender electric guitar. If I am not mistaken, I paid $212 for it. That guitar really got me playing more because the neck on it was so super. It just opened up a lot of things that you couldn't do on the others. None of the guitars I owned had a truss rod, and the action would get so high that I got calluses on my fingers to where you could have driven a ten-penny nail in them and it wouldn't have hurt! The Fender changed the whole outlook. All the other guitar manufacturers had to compete with them for the ease of the neck.

What part do your amps play in getting your sound?

A lot. I've gone through everything Kustom makes, and they've even made special things for me. It's really fascinating to me that the more sophisticated the equipment gets, the harder it gets for me to be pleased. I remember years back playing two guitars—a rhythm and a lead—through maybe a fivewatt Maestro amp with one ragged 12-inch speaker that danced around on the stage when we played. It sounded great to us at the time because we weren't comparing. Now you have so many ways to go with sound that you just get caught up in it. That has caused me more problems in the last five years than any other single thing—getting satisfied with the sound.

Do you have any problems switching between acoustic and electric during a set?

The fact that I do it a lot helps take the shock off. But it is different, and a lot of the jokes and raps that I do when I'm changing instruments are to give me a chance to sit there and adjust the volume, because I play strictly by sound. If it doesn't sound right, I'm gone. I can't play if the volume is too loud. I have to hold back on my picking, and I lose all my technique. If it is too soft, I have to hit it harder, and that gives me the same problem.

How do you gain speed in your playing?

For me, it's all in the wrist. My dad taught me that right away. If you use your wrist for your motion, there's almost no limit to how fast you can go. It's also flashier looking. A guitarist with a smooth technique can play faster than me, but the audience won't realize he's doing it. Meanwhile, I'm picking and the wrist is going and everybody thinks I'm really flying.

Are you a strict alternate up-down picker?

Yes. George Barnes was my idol. He would play with such drive and dynamics. There was a lot of controversy. They said, "George plays all downstrokes." That's impossible. They would go to him and say, "We know the secret of how you play," and he'd laugh at them. He played sort of conventional but with such great tone and feel. He played right on top of the beat, and I loved that.

Are there others you can point to as influences?

I've really been influenced by everyone. I have always said that you can learn from anyone that plays—regardless of how long they've been playing, what instrument they play, or how well they play it. If they play "themselves"—if it's "them"—you can learn something. They may hit the same lick that you did, but they're going to do it just a little bit different. They're not going to copy it exactly. They may think they are, but if they have any imagination, it's going to be just a little different. I've watched kids that have been playing two weeks and people who have been playing 50 years, and you can learn from all of them.

Can you think of any specific exercises that you could recommend to people that would be particularly helpful for developing technique?

One of the things that really helped me were fiddle tunes. If you learn a fiddle tune note-for-note from a good fiddle player or from a book, it will really help. Learn it note-for-note. Don't cheat on it. Don't do little slurs and things that you have a tendency to do if you're playing fast. Play it slow until you get it even, and just keep increasing the speed until you can play it as fast as you want. There are so many notes that it will really get your coordination down. To me, that is a good exercise, and it's not boring. You're actually playing something.

Do you listen to much music?

I don't get a chance. My life consists mostly of the inside of an airplane, the inside of a taxi or limousine, the inside of a motel room, and the inside of a concert hall. Very few motel rooms have radios, so you listen to what's on TV, which doesn't tell you much. I need to hear those things to excite my imagination and turn me on to new ideas.

What do you do when you go into the studio to record?

Panic, first. And then I just sit down and start getting into it. I don't go in often enough. When you're onstage, you just play, and if you blow a note it's gone. The technique gets sloppy, because even if you're recording the same tunes you're playing onstage, there are a lot of things you just don't hear. When you go into a studio and start picking and play it back, you hear all kinds of noises, creaks, grinds, and groans coming out of the guitar, and you suddenly realize that you are really going to have to get in there and work at it to get it clean again.

How much do you prepare before you go in to record?

Not at all. That's the way my recording career has been from the start. I've never dedicated myself and devoted the time to it. We've just walked in when we've had three days off and cut the record, and the albums sound exactly like that. Next year is going to be the first year that we are starting to try some creative things in recording. I want to take some time off and really put together an album that I've always wanted to do. Basically, it will be an instrumental album featuring some really hot guitar pieces in the vein of my earlier things. Something I can point to and say, "This is really what I'm capable of doing." Instead, now I play something and say, "Well, the engineers did a good job, and it's well mastered, and it's not bad sounding, but I know I can do better than that."

Do you have any records you really like?

None that I would honestly say contain my best work all the way through. I listen back to something, and I wonder why in the world I did it that way—where was my mind when I did that? I'm sure at the moment it seemed like I really wanted to play that, but that's the kind of thing you can avoid by taking your time and going over your music for like a six-month period. You come back a week later and listen, and if it still sounds good, you keep it. If not, you dump it and try again.

As something of a child whiz yourself, are you surprised to see so many young kids these days with amazing chops?

I think that's one of the greatest things to come out of the mid-'50s and early '60s—people were turned on to music. When I started playing, I wasn't a freak, but I was very unusual. A kid my age didn't play—except the ones in the school band. Now, a lot of young people are getting into playing.

How do you think time has affected your playing?

I must say that I am really subdued and settled compared to what I used to be. Success will do that to you, I guess. It turns your thinking around. You don't have that freedom—that pure gut feeling of just getting out and flailing it. You have a tendency to hold back and be more reserved, which takes away from your performance. I used to do things where I didn't know what I was doing. Now, I have an idea what I'm doing, but I'm afraid to do it. I hold back because I think it's tacky or doesn't mean anything anymore. Good guitar players used to come down and watch our shows when they got off work just to see this kid up there who was just so abandoned on the guitar. It would be good to play with that freedom again. —*Excerpted from the November 1978 issue of* Guitar Player

Zal Cleminson

BY MICHAEL MOLENDA | MAY 2008

DRESSED UP AS A MAD PUPPET IN WHITEFACE, YOU COULDN'T miss Zal Cleminson as he prowled stages with the Sensational Alex Harvey Band in the '70s. A glorious oddity of the times, Scotland's wackiest band merged theatrics, a self-made mythology ("Vambo Rool"), Cleminson's incredibly strange and lyrical riffs, and Harvey's almost unintelligible Scottish burr into a celebration of frenetic bombast. SAHB outlived its namesake, who passed away while on a solo tour in 1982, and, until Cleminson decided to retire from the stage in 2008, continued to tour with new vocalist Max Maxwell fronting original members Chris Glen (bass), Hugh McKenna (keyboards), and Ted McKenna (drums). Cleminson ended his SAHB career still in makeup and playing as stunning and as brutal as ever.

"If it ain't got feel," he explains, "you're pretty much screwed."

What was your classic gear, and what did you use just before you retired?

My classic SAHB gear was a '60s Gibson SG, a Marshall 100-watt head through a Vox Beatles cabinet, and no effects. Everything was stolen in Miami while touring with Jethro Tull, so I replaced it with a 100-watt Sunn stack and a Gibson Firebird. My most recent guitar was hand built by a guy in Glasgow named Graham Hypher. It's a Telecaster-style body that has been reshaped and sprayed black. It has a single EMG pickup and a single volume knob, and that's it. For what I do, it's perfect—loud as f**k and no frills! Graham christened it "The Angry Haggis." My amp was a Marshall Mode Four stack. For me, the perfect guitar tone is something that works for rhythm and lead, so I can simply adjust the guitar's volume knob for a clean sound or to get some overdrive for a solo. I used a Boss ME50 for effects, and my strings were any .010–.046 set.

Your riffs are so wonderfully bizarre. How did you develop that robotic intro for the SAHB tune "Vambo"?

That riff is loosely based on a chicken pickin' style. It's played very aggressively and rhythmically, and the wah sets up its own pulse along with the phrasing—like sequencing. The riff sounds hard, and it is. That's a sore one to play! I don't know why I used the wah, because I rarely use it at all. Dave [Batchelor, SAHB producer] may have suggested it. Typically, I start a riff or solo by playing what I hear in my head. It can be jaw-dropping or cataclysmic, but soon enough I get an idea, and I try to refine it. Of course, there are occasions when I don't want to refine it, so it stays somewhere in the *Twilight Zone*—totally inspired and spooky.

> *"Typically, I start a riff or solo by playing what I hear in my head."*

So what was the deal with the makeup?

In the '70s, that character was a big hit. It came about as a result of guitar angst and parody. The whiteface simply gave the audience a better view of what I was up to. I wore it in the last version of SAHB in homage to that formative legacy. Also, when you're all dressed up like a Christmas tree, and you hit the stage with the adrenalin flowing, the energy immediately takes over. The flashy crap all comes steaming out. It's too Spinal Tap at times, but I love all that prancing and showing off. If the technique suffers along the way, then ask Hendrix how he coped!

Larry Collins

BY DAN FORTE | AUGUST 1991

THE GUITAR WORLD HAS SEEN ITS SHARE OF CHILD PRODIGIES—
from James Burton to Charlie Sexton—but none compare to Larry Collins. Today,
he is a successful songwriter, with credits like Tanya Tucker's "Delta Dawn" and
Kenny Rogers' "You're the Reason God Made Oklahoma." But in February 1954,
he and older sister Lorrie, the Collins Kids, became regulars on the weekly *Town
Hall Party* TV show on Los Angeles' KTTT, less than a year after the Collins family
had moved from Tulsa.

The crew-cutted, rhinestone-outfitted Larry played hot guitar like a veteran, in
spite of the fact that he was only nine at the time, having picked up the guitar just
two years earlier. Dwarfed by a doubleneck Mosrite identical to the one *Town Hall*
costar Joe Maphis played, Larry nevertheless bounced like a yo-yo and spun like a
top, peeling off blistering solos on rockabilly classics like "Hoy Hoy," "Hop, Skip
and Jump," "Whistle Bait," and "Hurricane," one of his supercharged twin-guitar
workouts with Maphis.

Collins got his first guitar, a Stella acoustic, when he was about seven.

"I was a hyper little boy," he laughs. "When they first gave me that Stella, I could
play. I had a gift. But I jumped around like an idiot and did it about four times
faster than anybody else. Everybody laughed at me, so I took my BB gun and shot
my guitar. The first real guitar players I was exposed to were Merle Travis and Joe
Maphis, when I started on the TV show. I had the best godfathers in the world. Joe

and Merle were always helpful to me. If there was something I couldn't do, they'd show me real quick. And vice versa—some of my licks were so simple, they didn't understand them. So it kind of worked back and forth.

"We'd sit down and play back and forth, like it was automatic. I kind of knew what he was going to do, and he knew what I was going to do. When I was about nine, and we got a recording contract from CBS, he said, 'We'll write a song for you.' I said, 'Well, how do you go about that?' He said, 'You begin.' So that's how we came up with 'Hurricane.' I don't want to take away from practice—I used to practice seven or eight hours a day—but it didn't seem like practice. It was more creation—creating whatever the hell came out."

"I wasn't quite old enough to be a sex symbol, and when I did get to that age, the rock thing had already happened."

One piece of guitar showmanship on *Town Hall Party* featured Collins, Maphis, and Merle Travis all playing one Mosrite doubleneck.

"That wasn't really rehearsed, it was just, 'You grab this, I'll do this.' They were extraordinarily talented men. There was no insecurity around them."

Although the image of grown country artists jamming with a pintsized preadolescent grinning from ear to ear is an undeniable novelty attraction, Joe and Merle treated Larry like a peer.

"It was never, 'Let's take care of the kid,'" he explains. "Hell, I had the responsibility of an adult and was expected to act like one, and I never let them down."

Young Larry also came in contact with the King of the Surf Guitar, southpaw Dick Dale, who credits Collins as an influence.

"He used to date my sister," Larry points out. "He started on *Town Hall Party* doing the amateur show. It was kind of humorous at first because he had his guitar strung backwards. I said, 'You've got 'em going bass-ackwards.' But he was always real nice to me, and he was a talented guy. I used to sit around and teach him stuff. They'd wake me up after they got home from a date and go, 'Now, Larry, how does this lick go?'"

Larry had his first huge songwriting success in 1971, when he cowrote "Delta Dawn." He credits Mac Davis with steering him toward writing seriously. Other artists who have recorded his tunes include Lou Rawls, Henry Mancini, Bette Midler, Waylon Jennings, Willie Nelson, Helen Reddy, and Merle Haggard. He's also responsible for several soundtrack selections from *Smokey and the Bandit II*, *Every Which Way but Loose*, and *Any Which Way You Can* (whose "You're the Reason God

Made Oklahoma" was voted 1982 Song of the Year by the Academy of Country Music and the Nashville Songwriters Association).

Collins moved to Reno in '88, where he lives with his wife, Margie. Lorrie, who is currently in the real estate business, also lives in Reno. Thanks to the rockabilly revival of the early '80s, the Collins Kids are now viewed as an important part of the genre.

"We did something nobody had ever heard before," says Larry. "I think it all had to do with my being so hyper, and the Pentecostal black music that influenced me back then. I liked the beat."

Another factor in the Collins Kids' unjust obscurity is the fact that CBS marketed them as a wholesome country act. After all, they were regulars on a TV show hosted by Tex Ritter. Also, as Larry points out, "I wasn't quite old enough to be a sex symbol, and when I did get to that age, the rock thing had already happened. However, what we did with the music kind of inspired a lot of that, and it gave more of an opportunity to the other guys who had that image and were a little older."

Looking back on his past and present achievements, Collins is justifiably proud.

"It pleases me that it kind of caught up with itself, and people like the Stray Cats gave me and Lorrie credit," he smiles. "I don't know if we were first, but we were pretty damn close to it." —*Excerpted from the August 1991 issue of* Guitar Player

Reeves Gabrels

BY MICHAEL MOLENDA | MAY 2000

"I DON'T HAVE ANY DESIRE TO PROVE OR DISPROVE CHOPS,"

asserts Reeves Gabrels. "I just want to raise goosebumps on someone's neck."

These are scary words coming from a player celebrated as a blatantly eccentric aural iconoclast. Even more perplexing are the conventional compositions and Beatles-esque melodies that grace his latest solo venture, *Ulysses (della notte)*. But like Gabrels' junk-adorned Parker Nitefly, there's plenty of weird stuff pasted to his pop songs. Massively distorted, dolphin-like chatters, horror-movie shrieks, and vortexes of modulated, pissed-off hornet armadas are just some of the bizarre guitar timbres that keep *Ulysses* from being confused with a Hanson record.

"It's actually a fairly confessional singer/songwriter album," offers Gabrels, as he strums a newly acquired Les Paul Junior in the Riviera kitsch of his room at San Francisco's Hotel Monaco. "For me, melody is the last frontier. It's really more dangerous than composing stuff that's out on the edge, because you're putting your emotions—and the most vulnerable side of your ego—on the line. Melody is not about flash or blistering sounds; it's about communicating what you feel in your heart. And, man, just saying *that* to somebody can make you feel a little queasy."

Considering all its layered melodicism, sonic complexity, and downright strangeness, the fact that much of *Ulysses* was produced and recorded by Gabrels in his home studio suggests an impressive arrangement sense. "The production thing and the guitar thing meld for me," he says. "I'm not just writing parts—I always try to

develop sonic landscapes. If I can create something that gives me pictures, then I can inspire lyrics. And once I have lyrics, the song is on its way."

To create the "pictures" for *Ulysses*, Gabrels assembled a fleet of digital and tube gear. "I used anything and everything from a SansAmp to a Korg Pandora to a Mesa/ Boogie Dual Rectifier head running through a Marshall or Groove Tubes speaker emulator and straight into the board," explains Gabrels. "If there was a tonal hole to fill, I'd just figure out what it would take. For example, an AC30 or a Boogie Mark II would be thickened up by layering a Marshall stack sound, and I might add dimension to the Pandora by doubling a part using a Fender Champ miked with an SM57. Then I'd use my Roland VG-8 to fill in any blanks, or provide vintage-type sounds such as a Telecaster and B-Bender combination. For the more heinous stuff, I usually plugged my Parker into a Z.Vex Fuzz Factory, the Pandora, and a Boogie Heartbreaker with a Boogie 2x12 cab. It's like the Jimmy Page thing, where you blend all these sounds that might sound crappy by themselves, but the interlocking sound is great. Even hiss becomes part of the aural effect."

> *"Melody is not about flash or blistering sounds; it's about communicating what you feel in your heart."*

An important component of the record-making process was Digidesign's Pro Tools. The hard-disk recording software is vilified in some quarters for "saving" less-than-stellar players due to its ability to cut and paste lame performances into respectability.

"Look, I'm a rock-based improviser, and Pro Tools lets me do what I do best— *play*," he says. "I can work on a song and basically piss all over the track, then find the cool stuff and put it where I want. And it's really a thrill playing through an entire song, rather than just working on the solo section. I like responding to things in the verses and choruses. Often I'll stumble into a cool lick or phrase a line in an interesting way. Those parts—which I might *never* have played if I was concentrating on a 'solo'—can be used to construct extremely cool lead lines or signature riffs. Now if you devote eight hours a day to practicing, it's really hard to let that go, and Pro Tools may seem like an abomination. But I view guitarists like barbarians with broadswords. We need to be good with the instrument, but we also have to know when it's time to do whatever it takes to survive."

Rory Gallagher

BY STEFAN GROSSMAN | MARCH 1978

BLUES IS SAID TO BE A UNIVERSAL EXPERIENCE—AS ALBERT

King once preached, "Everybody understands the blues"—and Rory Gallagher is sure-
ly a case in point. Born in Ballyshannon, County Donegal, Ireland, Rory at first at-
tempted to play cowboy songs and Irish folk tunes on acoustic guitar beginning at age
nine. American rock and rollers such as Buddy Holly, Eddie Cochran, Elvis Presley,
and Chuck Berry made an early impression on Rory, though he discovered blues—a la
Leadbelly and Woody Guthrie—by way of Lonnie Donegan's British skiffle hits.

At 15, Gallagher joined the Fontana Show Band, which toured England and Ireland. The constant work helped refine Rory's playing, but the commercial nature of
the repertoire caused him to look elsewhere for artistic satisfaction. In 1965, Rory
formed Taste, the now legendary blues-rock trio comprised of Eric Kitteringham on
bass, Norman Damery on drums, and Gallagher on guitar, vocals, and, occasionally,
saxophone. Though the power trio preceded Cream by several years, comparisons
with the English supergroup were inevitable.

In 1969, Taste signed with Polydor Records, but by 1970, it had disbanded, and
Rory pursued a solo career. To date, Gallagher has appeared on over 20 albums, either as leader or sideman, and has graced sessions featuring such notables as Muddy
Waters, Jerry Lee Lewis, and Albert King. What Gallagher has to say about blues
and rock and roll should be required reading for any aspiring guitarists, just as his
many records and live performances should be required listening.

When you're performing, don't you consider yourself mainly a blues-oriented musician?

Yes, I do, but I think that I've always strived to forge ahead. At some point, when I'm 40 or 50, I hope I'll have a very distinct sound, as Elmore or Muddy did, so that when you turn on the radio—*that's* Rory Gallagher. It's a thin line between studying the blues and listening to an awful lot of it on one hand, and loving the stuff and doing some blues numbers in your own style on the other hand. It's hard to break it down into percentages, because some nights we might do something like "Messing with the Kid," a well known Junior Wells song, or "Bullfrog Blues," or "Rag Mama," the Blind Boy Fuller tune. By the songs I pick to do, you can see the kind of people I like.

Your changes of style seem to depend in part upon what instrument you are playing. Whereas you seem to lean toward a lot of the acoustic ragtime blues people, when you play electric, you go into a completely different area of blues music.

Well, I'm a great fan of all the Kings—the Alberts, the B. B.s, and the Freddies. I wouldn't want to say that these people have been overrated, because that would be an absolute insult, but I think they've been recognized to the point where the Earl Hookers and Hubert Sumlins have been underrated. And the guitar player who was with Wolf before Sumlin, Willie Johnson, was a hot player as well.

What do you use for an electric guitar?

I have two different electrics. I have a Fender Stratocaster with Fender lightgauge Rock and Roll strings, which I use for basic playing and some slide work in straight tuning. I also have a Fender Telecaster for A tuning and other open tunings.

Why the Stratocaster?

Well, that's the eternal argument among Fender fans. Buddy Holly had a Strat, and as a child you go after the appearance of a guitar. I don't care what anyone says. You look at the shape of the thing, and that's it. I've tried Gibsons, but I'm not a great fan of humbucking pickups.

Why is that?

Because as you bring down the volume from 10 to 9 to 8, after that—forget it, the guitar loses its sensitivity and drive. Whereas with the single-coil or P-90 pickups, the volume control goes down nice and gradually, and even at 6 the guitar is still doing something. I like a good bright tone, and I like the out-of-phase sound you can get with the switch set between the normal positions on a Strat. It's comfortable, the scale seems right, and I like having the machine heads on one side—it just seems to make sense. But if you want, say, a more luxurious, fatter sound, the Gibson guitar certainly would do the job.

Is your Strat modified in any way?

It's practically straight off the rack. The only modification is that the Tone control

for the middle pickup is now a Master Volume control, because, over the years, I've found that when you jump from the middle pickup to the lead, or treble, pickup, you couldn't adjust it.

Why do you usually switch to the Telecaster for slide?

I thought it had a certain steel-guitar type of tone that would work well with slide, but I was frustrated with the rhythm pickup. I thought it was too thin. So I put a Strat pickup there, and it remained that way for a year. Then I said, "To hell with it. I'll do the Telecaster a la Strat." So now I've got two Strat pickups and a Tele lead pickup and a five-way Strat toggle switch. It's like the best of both worlds with the Telecaster lead pickup, which is slightly hotter than a Stratocaster's.

Is it strung the same as the Stratocaster?

No, it's kind of a blend. I have something like an .013 for the first, then .015, an unwound .018, and so on. On the Strat, it's as they come out of the packet: .010, .012, .015, .026, .032, .038. That seems to be about the most balanced set I could find. I would prefer something like an .040 on the bottom—which I sometimes stick on if I have it handy—because I think the bottom end is a little too light for me.

Is the action higher on the Telecaster for the slide work?

The action on the Strat is quite high, as well. I like a high action—like on an acoustic.

What do you use for a slide?

It depends. I shift around. I sometimes use a bottleneck on my ring finger for electric stuff. Otherwise, I've got two stainless steel tubes, which I sometimes use on my small finger or the ring finger. They get a more stinging, Muddy Waters sound. You get a different sound depending on what slide you use. For instance, if you're playing slide on a National with a glass slide, forget it. You have to have something like steel, or, even better, copper. Son House used copper, and I've got one of those, as well.

Were these slides store-bought items, or did you just go to a hardware shop?

I went to a hardware shop, got the proverbial bit of piping chopped up, and got a Brillo pad out and shone it up. There's a bit of surface noise there, but Son House has that sound. It's best because it clings to the strings. I used to use copper on electric as well, but I found that the stainless steel was a pretty good compromise between the copper or bronze and the glass. Glass is nice because it works a little more like a Hawaiian or lap-steel guitar—it's sweeter and softer. I change my mind every couple of gigs.

What type of amplification do you use?

For years, I used a Vox AC30—which is the best all-around European amp I've ever come across. I still have it. The Shadows used to use them, and the Beatles used them, so you know it was the popular amp. But I found that when using the treble booster you got a built-in gain, because the transistors were fairly primitive. If I used the Normal input—which was very bassy as opposed to the Brilliant input—I could get that nice rough edge without getting into a very fuzzy sound. I used that for years, and I've had odds and sods in between, but then I moved on to an old '50s tweed Fender Twin, which I still have. Then I got into a tweed Fender Bassman, and recently I got a Fender Concert—an old brown one, from around 1959, with four 10" speakers. I use a Hawk booster through that just to roughen it up a bit, or if it's a quiet number, I plug straight in and keep the guitar clean sounding.

"You have to direct your playing somewhere— unless you want to sit in a room like the painter looking at the painting he's just done, and he won't show it to anybody."

For those wanting to be professional guitarists, do you feel that playing in front of people is an important thing to do as soon as possible?

Yes, it brings something out. I know for a fact that if I'm off the road for a long spell—even if I'm rehearsing like mad and playing a lot at home—the real crunch comes when I get out in front of people. The things you thought were really hot in rehearsal don't make any sense, because, quite often, you've forgotten the basic drive. In rehearsals, sometimes the basics get glossed over because you're fooling around too much with the frilly stuff. If you get out there in front of an audience, drop your pick or break a string, it toughens you up, and it brings out projection in your playing. You have to direct your playing somewhere—unless you want to sit in a room like the painter looking at the painting he's just done, and he won't show it to anybody.

In addition, there's always a thin line between studying the old records by the old masters and trying to develop yourself. I think both can be done at the same time, because if you forget the old masters you miss out on a whole heritage and a whole world, really. But you shouldn't get too clogged up with the old stuff to the point where you won't be moving on yourself. —*Excerpted from the March 1978 issue of* Guitar Player

Neil Giraldo

BY MICHAEL MOLENDA |
GUITARPLAYER.COM, MAY 2004

ALTHOUGH HE IS NEARING THE HALF-CENTURY MARK,
Cleveland-born Neil Giraldo hasn't lost even one tiny molecule of his celebrated intensity and swagger. The chugging, churning onslaught of guitar that helped propel his musical and life partner Pat Benatar toward mega-hit status in 1979 and beyond remains unbowed in the new millennium. This is a man who loves to play and who loves to play *hard*.

What's your main guitar at the moment?

I use GMP guitars. I don't have a Spyder model or anything like that, but they've made a few different guitars for me. I usually ask for P-90 pickups, but I have some humbucker models for live shows. You know, onstage with lighting rigs and dimmer racks and everything—well, P-90s aren't really happy with some of that kind of stuff. But normally, I go for P-90 models, and that's usually what I record with. I also ask for a Bigsby and locking tuners.

What about amplifiers?

Onstage, I use a Line 6 Pod and a Line 6 Flextone combo. I like the two devices working together, because the Pod reacts a couple of milliseconds after you attack the note, which actually helps fatten up the sound a bit more. For effects, I go with the onboard models. I don't use any pedals. In the studio, I may use my Marshall combo. I crank the Master Volume and keep Volume at about 12 o'clock. If I need

to drive the amp a little bit more, I stick in a Fulltone Full-Drive 2 to drive the front end a little harder. I don't use it as a distortion pedal—just as a preamp.

What about strings?

I use D'Addario strings. I go with .012–.058, sometimes .060. Pretty thick. I go with the highest *G* I can get that isn't wound, and I tune to *E♭*. If I do tune to *E*, I'll swap out the high stings for a .011 set, but I'll keep the heavy gauges on the low strings, because I like to hit the low strings pretty hard, and I don't want them to go out of tune.

To me, one of the most identifiable aspects of your style is your slightly snackered rhythm-guitar approach. It seems that you like to push and pull the groove and sometimes throw surprises into your rhythmic accents. Where did that come from?

I don't know, but I'm glad you picked up on it, because I love to play rhythm guitar more than anything. I love rhythm so much. I think it has to do with the fact that I'm a frustrated drummer. When I was a kid, I would play drums to Simon and Garfunkel records because they never really had any drums on them, and I would try to find a way to get inside the rhythms they did.

Another odd thing is that I could never figure out parts from records exactly the way they were played. I'd get, say, a Yardbirds song, and I could

> *"It's about doing whatever it takes to move people and keep them involved in the song from start to finish."*

sort of learn it, but I'd end up putting my own spin—my own little parts—into the mix until it really didn't sound much like the parts on the record.

So you weren't exactly the best cat to pick for a cover band, then?

No—I was terrible [*laughs*]. When I was playing in local bands when I was a kid, people didn't want me in their groups because they were looking for someone who could play *straighter*. There would always have to be another guitar player in the band who would play the correct parts. It's goofy, but I guess I was never interested to do things the "right" way. I'd be thinking, "You know, I think they should have played this part instead."

How do you conceptualize a groove for a song?

I think of the rhythm, the drums, the tempo, the swing, or the "roll," as I call it. But, again, I don't think about it too much. I just do it. And, you know, on all the records I've ever done, I've always kept the guitar and drums going down together at once. I would never, ever overdub my rhythm guitar. I'd have to play live with the drums to get my parts to work together.

Who are some of your favorite rhythm guitarists?

Pete Townshend—definitely. I also love Jimi Hendrix. When I would listen to his stuff on vinyl, I would skip over the solos because I didn't care about them. Give me any song on *Axis: Bold as Love*. Listen to that rhythm stuff!

You have a very aggressive rock-guitar sound, but it never seems to get in your lead singer's way.

Yeah. I don't know how to explain that. I don't know why that happens [*laughs*]. Honestly, I don't know. I know that if I start thinking about it, I'll f**k up. I know that for a fact. I also know that I hate to be a selfish player. I hate to be a selfish producer or arranger. I don't like saying, "Hey, look at me! Look what I can do." What I'm trying to create in arrangements is the song people want to hear. People want to hear the song, and they want to hear the singer. My job is to make sure it feels great, and that it's going right to their blood, and that it's going to rip their heart out.

From a guitar standpoint, what's the most important thing to ensuring a song rips someone's heart out when they hear it?

Your playing should really start accelerating so that when you listen to the end of the song, it sounds like the end of the song is coming. It shouldn't sound like the beginning. What worries me, with all the recording tools that people have, is that they will take a part they like—something that feels good—and paste it throughout the whole song. That's the part of the guitar thing you have to be really, really careful about. You shouldn't miss the idea that the end of the song should really be a little quicker and more intense than the beginning. The intensity level should be changing, and I don't think a lot of people understand that. It's about doing whatever it takes to *move* people and keep them involved in the song from start to finish.

Speaking of intensity, you haven't lost any fire from when I first saw you onstage back in 1980. Many players tend to cool off a bit with time. How have you kept up the enthusiasm and the energy?

I think, mainly, it was a change I made in my life. I was smoking three packs of cigarettes a day, drinking way too much Irish whiskey, and just living that lifestyle. You know—doing stuff to way too much excess. I finally said to myself, "Wait a second. I have children, and I'm getting too old for this. I've got to look hard at what I'm doing here. I've got to take care of myself." So I started a serious physical routine that I thought I'd never be able to do. I went from being able to run 20 feet to running six miles a day. Now, I can jump rope for 20 minutes straight. I lift weights. I do all kinds of physical stuff. This has been going on for the last seven years, and I think it is what gives me the energy and the attitude. If I wasn't doing the exercise, I don't know if I'd still be able to be as physical and in-your-face as a player—and that kind of player is the player I still want to be.

Well, that mental approach seems huge. Perhaps some players start thinking, "Hey, I'm 50 years old—I can't be jumping up and down anymore. It's not fitting."

I don't give a sh*t about that. I call it, "last man standing." Anybody who knows me knows that I'm relentless. If someone tells me I can't do something, I will do everything in my power to show you that I can. It's a philosophy I try to live by, and I try to instill it in my children, as well. My playing is no different, because the tone is in my hands and the attitude is in my heart, and I can't change that. Even though you may be getting old, unless something is physically affecting what you're able to do, you should stay pretty consistent performance-wise—as long as you're ruthless enough [*laughs*].

Do you feel you've gotten your due in the guitar-culture world, or do you care about that kind of stuff?

I did care for a while when I was younger. It doesn't matter to me now. In the mid-'80s, I was doing just about everything—arranging, producing, playing, and so on. It was really my band, but I don't think anyone knew that or gave me props for everything I was doing to help craft all the hits. The wife and myself were equal partners—we still are—but I didn't understand why management decided not to do anything to promote the *band*. But, you know, I get it, and right now it means very little to me whether audiences focus directly on my contributions. It's far more important that I do great work, and that somebody appreciates the great work—whether they know my name or not.

John Goodsall

BY TOM MULHERN | AUGUST 1980

JOHN GOODSALL WAS BORN ON FEBRUARY 15, 1953, IN

London and grew up in nearby Surrey. Although his grandmother was a singer, young John's greatest influence was his grandfather, a bandleader who played mostly piano but doubled with guitar, reed instruments, and trumpet, and was classically trained on violin. His musicality left a lasting impression on Goodsall. By the time he was seven years old, John had a guitar—a Rossetti Lucky 7 acoustic that cost about £7.

"I didn't even know how to tune it," he recalls. "I used to have my own tunings. One of them called for every string to be set a major second above the adjacent one."

For Christmas that year, John received a Vox Broadway electric, which his father had had tuned before bringing it home from the music store.

"He said, 'That's how you tune it.' I picked it up and noticed that the E and B were tuned to a fourth. What a difference. Straightaway, I set out to learn one of my favorite tunes, 'Apache,' by the Shadows. I picked out the notes and played right through it, almost immediately."

Goodsall progressed from playing in his room to working out songs with friends in small bands. By the time he reached his teens, John was traveling with groups more frequently, and his absence from school became almost commonplace.

"I was thrown out of school when I was 15—one term early—even though I was planning to leave anyway. I was touring with a band called Babylon. We went all over for two years."

Eventually, John joined the heavy-metal group Atomic Rooster, with whom he recorded one album, *Nice and Greasy.*

"That was the first hard rock gig I ever did," he says, "and it took some getting used to. After all, I was coming from a sort of laid-back, R&B jazz background. We were smashing up equipment and getting crazy all the time, and we all went under tongue-in-cheek spiritual pseudonyms. I was Johnny Mandala."

In his two-and-a-half years with Atomic Rooster, Goodsall went through several guitars. He found that his Gibson ES-335 presented too many feedback problems when used at high volume levels. John switched to a Gibson SG Standard, but he thought the body was too thin.

"So I had [luthier] Tony Zemaitis build a Les Paul-type solidbody with a couple of humbuckers. It was really plain—not like some of his fancy carved jobs. I also got a Gibson Firebird, but because we used to get crazy onstage, I ended up breaking the neck off."

After Atomic Rooster disbanded, John Goodsall found himself playing in London's bars doing various kinds of copy material. He also started edging into studio work, and while at Island Studios, he met Percy Jones and Robin Lumley. Their mutual interest in jazz led to a decision to work together. The partnership eventually evolved into a four-piece unit without vocals, and Brand X was launched.

Since Brand X's earliest days, John has used a 1974 Fender Stratocaster, and although it has a vibrato, he has only recently begun using it. His other onstage guitars are two Washburn Falcons and a Shergold 6/ 12 double-neck.

"I like the Washburns," he explains. "They're really powerful."

With his electrics, John uses a Burman amp—a British model that he describes as similar to a Mesa/Boogie. On tour in the States, he uses a Mesa/Boogie combo with a single 15-inch speaker. Between the guitar and amp only a few effects are used.

"I have a Boss Chorus, and occasionally I'll use a Mu-Tron Flanger, but in general I'm not too keen about putting anything between the guitar and amp. You just add more noise to the signal. So I always make sure that the pedals I get don't degrade the quality of the signal."

Primarily a rock guitarist before joining Brand X, Goodsall has encountered no difficulties in adapting to a jazz-rock forum or in communicating with his comrades. And because he and Percy Jones are the steadiest members of Brand X, they determine much of its musical direction.

"This isn't to say we're the leaders," John explains. "It's just that we're there all the time. No one's the leader—except the person who wrote the tune we're working on. And everyone writes for the band. Naturally, the writer will want to hear certain things his way. Percy is still writing more progressive, modal things that use odd time signatures, whereas I'm going the other way—into a more 4/4-oriented scheme with conventional chords. This is probably because I'm into songs. And as odd as it may seem, I get bored ten times faster with jazz-rock than I did with rock. You get tired of playing thirty-second notes two sets a night."

In 1978, those high-speed precision lines that Goodsall found a drudge took their toll. He was laid up for 18 months because of tendonitis in his right arm. He had to take it easy and was told to keep his arm in a sling for the duration. Meanwhile, a stand-in guitarist went out on Brand X's tour.

"When the arm was getting bad," John says, "I could get through the set, but I just couldn't do certain parts of "The Poke" very well. You know, the sixteenth-notes, wide-interval jumps, and stuff like that. I didn't like having my arm in a sling. That was even more uncomfortable than the tendonitis. Instead, I started lifting weights to build up my muscles. Now that I'm a lot stronger, I've had no recurring problems with the tendonitis. I'm now writing things that are more in the straight-ahead rock vein in order to avoid things that are too challenging."

"And as odd as it may seem, I get bored ten times faster with jazz-rock than I did with rock."

Steadfastly a member of Brand X, Goodsall feels no urge to become a studio great, even though he is always striving to expand his abilities. He only accepts occasional dates in which he is free to play his own style of music.

"I don't even get asked unless it's a really interesting session," he says. "Robin Lumley or someone at our management will sometimes come up with one that will allow me to play my own way. So I don't do a lot of sessions. I don't really want to. I just wouldn't want to settle into doing an endless succession of disco and pop gigs. That would just be work, as far as I'm concerned."

Juliana Hatfield

BY DARRIN FOX | OCTOBER 2000

WITH HER TWO NEW ALBUMS, *BEAUTIFUL CREATURE* AND
Total System Failure, Juliana Hatfield offers two contrasting—and convincing—musical statements. *Beautiful Creature* is possibly Hatfield's most focused collection of material ever and reestablishes her as one of rock's most intriguing songsmiths. Although
her elegantly tough—and at times pugnacious—guitar playing defers to the almighty
song, *Beautiful Creature* is soaked with cool tones and melodic riffs. But after complet-
ing the relatively mellow *Creature*, Hatfield was eager to explore her dark side.

"I wanted to play a ton of guitar and make a no-nonsense rock album," she says.
"So I recruited some perfectly unpolished rock guys to make the record I wanted to
make—a down-and-dirty rock album with an organic feel."

Adopting the moniker Juliana's Pony, the "unpolished" band—Hatfield, bassist
Mikey Welsh (of Weezer), and drummer Zephan Courtney—recorded Total System
Failure. This jarring, two-fisted disc features extended solos and unbelievably heavy,
saturated guitar tones, while still manifesting Hatfield's uncanny pop sensibilities.

**Was it tough switching gears from the relatively tame *Beautiful Creature* to the
sonic assault of *Total System Failure*?**

It felt completely natural. It's kind of scary—maybe I have split personalities. The
big difference with *Total System Failure* was that I made two rules that the band and
I had to follow. One: no love songs. Two: Each song had to have at least one guitar
solo—preferably, a long one.

Why more solos?

I was venting the side of me that didn't get expressed on *Beautiful Creature*. There is plenty of guitar on that record, but it takes a backseat to the presentation of each song. On *Total System Failure*, I wanted to see what I was capable of doing on guitar with no holds barred.

Your guitar-solo-on-every-tune ethos is contrary to what's happening now in modern rock.

I know, and that's too bad. I think the guitar solo needs to come back.

Are your solos improvised?

Usually, I do a couple of takes and gather ideas. Then I try to develop some of those ideas into a melodic theme. Occasionally, I'll comp different solos together.

What's your philosophy on soloing?

Save the mistakes—they're usually the best part. Many times, the greatest ideas are contained in takes where I thought I had completely messed up.

Do you go back and relearn the mistakes?

Sometimes, I'll relearn the original idea, but other times, the tape will capture something that is so weird and cool that you could *never* play it the same way again. In fact, I'm now trying to learn some of my *Total System Failure* solos for the tour, and it's tough recapturing the same vibe.

"Save the mistakes— they're usually the best part."

How has your guitar playing grown?

I have a lot more confidence now—I'm less afraid to take chances. And I've learned to relax, let the music breathe, and not walk all over everything. I've learned that I don't always need to be doing something. A lot of the coolest guitar moments are when you're *not* playing.

What was the reason for using different players on each album?

I viewed *Beautiful Creature* as an opportunity to experiment. I wanted to see what would happen if I used new elements—like a different guitarist and drum loops.

Did you find yourself playing differently with drum loops as opposed to a real drummer?

Definitely—it's a whole different energy. With loops, I tend to play with a lighter touch. With a real drummer, I feel more physically involved with my guitar playing. For me, the jury's still out on drum loops.

What gear did you use in the studio?

"Meat and potatoes" is how I describe my sound—just the essentials. For *Total System Failure*, I used my Gibson SG Firebrand, an Ibanez Tube Screamer, an Electro-Harmonix Big Muff [*Editor's note: Both pedals are usually on at the same time*], and an Ampeg Super Jet. I used to record with a Marshall and a 4x12 cabinet, but now I dig recording with little amps. They make the Big Muff sound more extreme. For *Beautiful Creature*, I plugged my SG—and occasionally an Epiphone Coronet—into the Super Jet or a Vox AC30. My acoustic guitar was a Gibson J-45.

You know, a lot of times, I just plug in and don't even know what I'm running through. I go into the control room and listen, and if it sounds good, I hit the Record button and go for it.

What comes first when you're writing?

It's usually a chord progression or riff, then a melody, and then lyrics.

How do you demo your songs?

What I usually do is record guitar and vocals into my Walkman. If I want to get more complex, I'll play that tape back on my boom box, put another tape into my Walkman, and record myself singing or playing along with the first tape. It's low-tech multitracking! I hardly ever use my 4-track because it's too much work. If I'm going to spend that much energy recording, I'd rather wait until I'm in the studio doing the real track.

Did you write differently for *Total System Failure*?

Partly. I had some songs finished when we went in the studio, and other ones were written on the spot. "Let's Get Married" is a good example of writing in the studio. I was messing around while the guys took a break, and I finished the song in about five minutes. When the guys came back, I showed it to them and we recorded it. Then I took it home and wrote the lyrics. Another way I generated new songs was jamming at home and coming up with a bunch of dumb riffs. I had Mikey do the same, and when we got to the studio, we put our ideas together to form complete songs. We wrote four tunes that way.

Have you ever worked like that before?

No—it was a new way for me. It was really great to realize that songwriting doesn't always have to be a painstakingly agonizing process.

How do you spark your creativity?

I don't need to. If I don't write for a long time, I just accept it as a break and don't worry about it. Inspiration comes in waves, and that's fine. I don't believe in writer's block. You simply go through periods where you don't like everything you write. It doesn't mean you stop. Keep going until you get to the good stuff, because that *will* eventually happen.

Hollywood Fats

BY DAN FORTE | SEPTEMBER 1977

WHEN ONE HEARS OF HIS CREDENTIALS AND THE HIGH
praise fellow musicians reserve for him, it usually comes as a surprise to find that
Mike Mann—affectionately known in blues circles as Hollywood Fats—is white and
a mere 23 years old. His professional career has already included stints with such
legendary names as Muddy Waters, John Lee Hooker, Albert King, Shakey Jake, J.
B. Hutto, and Jimmy Witherspoon. After his band opened for Lightnin' Hopkins at
the Lighthouse in Hermosa Beach, California, Lightnin' called them the best blues
band he'd heard in 15 years. Unfortunately, because of record companies' aversion
to anything called "blues," Fats and his band have yet to be recorded.

How did you first get into blues?

I started playing guitar when I was about ten, but I didn't really get into the instrument because there wasn't a style of music that I enjoyed enough to put an effort into
learning how to play it. Then, when I started hearing blues records, I really loved it. A
few years later, Freddie King played the Ash Grove in Los Angeles, and I sat in. Curtis
Tillman, who was playing bass with him, said, "You bad. I'm gonna get you some gigs
where people's gonna dig you." So he got me this regular gig down at 154th and Ava-
lon in Watts, a place called the Hideaway Lounge, and I ran into T-Bone Walker, Pee
Wee Crayton, Albert Collins—all the blues guys who were living here. I was 14. I just
got by on my playing. As long as I could play before people got a chance to get unruly,
then they loved me. I got a few wine bottles chucked at me after I got off work [*laughs*].

Did any of the older players show you things on the guitar?

Sure. The cats I've learned the most from technically would be Freddie King and Magic Sam. They were the ones who really sat me down and said, "Look, I know where you're coming from, but try doing this instead of this."

When backing a particular blues singer, do you make a conscious effort to play a certain way to fit his style?

Definitely, because in blues there are a lot of different styles, and I really like them all. The main reason I left Muddy Waters' band was because I really take pride in having learned how to play that music in the proper way, but I find that most of the cats playing with him don't put any effort into trying to get that old sound. It just doesn't have the fire anymore. It was just an emotional strain every night, going to work and trying to get that sound with the cat who *invented* it and not being able to. Everyone in the band is just cranking out that same bass line and is really apprehensive to throw in any fills or put any punch into it. And now, as with all blues cats, every slow blues or shuffle is just one patented part—or one line—that everybody plays for *all* slow blues and shuffles. Whereas, when those songs originally came out—even the ones which were really similar, like "Long Distance Call" and "Honey Bee" and "Standin' Around Crying"—each had unique things that made it tough. As far as my own style is concerned, it's a Chicago blues format, but I incorporate a little bit of swing and a lot of West Coast blues into it, too.

> *"If you're going to call something blues, just let it be blues."*

What equipment are you using?

I have two Gibson ES-345s—a '59 and a '63. One is stereo, one is mono, and one had the Varitone taken out. I also use an old Gibson L-4 that belongs to a friend of mine. I like it for that West Memphis, late-'40s, Willie Johnson and Willie Lacy kind of stuff. Sometimes I use it for, like, a late '40s or early '50s Chicago sound, but for single-string things it doesn't cut through enough. I use the 345 most of the time, because I think the full box sounds too foreign to most people. My amp's a Harmony 415 run through a Fender Reverb unit.

Do you foresee going into a different style? Getting into rock or funk things, instead of sticking with blues?

I like to shy away from that stuff, because I feel there are already enough people playing that way. I'd rather put the effort into more neglected areas. Rather than playing tunes with a funk beat, I'd prefer to pick out of all the old stuff the songs that have the most "contemporary" feel. I think a lot of the reason why blues isn't popular is that people aren't as picky as they should be when they present it. You'll hear a mediocre blues artist play five slow blues numbers, and naturally, someone who has never heard blues before isn't going to dig it.

What do you think of the commercialization of blues?

Now the blacks are all trying to sound like white kids, so you've got to get white kids who are trying to sound like blacks [*laughs*]. The reason blues isn't successful is that every attempt that's made at it, they're always changing it. They're not trying to do the real sh*t—they're trying to make it something else. Naturally, if what you're doing varies too much in sound from what it was originally, you can't play the same things. What complements one sound isn't going to complement another. And you can take older ideas and concepts and incorporate those into more contemporary styles to an extent, but when you try to take new things and put those into older styles, there's no context. I like contemporary stuff, but there's a certain limit, I think, before it gets outside of what's still considered blues. If you're going to call something blues, just let it be blues. Don't put a label on something that doesn't connote that name.

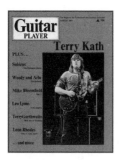

Terry Kath

BY JIM CROCKETT | AUGUST 1971

EVERYONE HAS HEARD OF CHICAGO—THE MOST POPULAR
band in the country—but how many know of the Big Thing or the Missing Links?
The Big Thing and the Missing Links and Chicago are *all* part of Terry Kath—one
of the most frequently requested guitarists in *GP*'s history.

Terry was born in Chicago, Illinois, 25 years ago. By the eighth grade, he had been
pounding on his older brother's drums for a year. His mother had a banjo around
the house, and Terry gravitated toward it, retuning it to sound like a guitar.

In the ninth grade, Terry got hold of a Kay guitar and amp and took up with a local kid band, copying every Ventures record they could get their hands on. No gigs,
but a lot of fun and experience. Three years later, the self-taught guitarist felt it was
time for some lessons, so he spent a year with a jazz teacher.

"He just kept wanting me to play good lead stuff," Terry recalls, "but, then, all I
wanted to do was play those rock and roll chords."

Dick Clark was big then. He had a massive TV show and also had two tours on
the road simultaneously as the Dick Clark Show. A friend of Terry's was playing
lead with the second group and told him there was an opening—for a bass player. A
newly acquired Fender Jazz Bass in hand, Kath took to the road for a year.

Terry still played bass when he met Chicago drummer Danny Seraphine, and they
formed a group called the Missing Links to play the area's many bars.

"The band was doing pretty well," he says, "so we thought we had to have a manager. This guy kept telling us that rock was the big thing, so he made us change the name to 'the Big Thing.' Can you believe that?"

They practiced for three or four months with Terry back to guitar and then started playing everything from Tijuana Brass to Hendrix. James William Guercio, the former bassist with Clark's other road band, was by then producing records in Los Angeles for groups like Blood, Sweat and Tears. He, as well as the members of the band, knew their future was limited in Chicago. Now called Chicago Transit Authority, they were expanding their music to reflect the members' various interests in classical music and jazz.

"I'm too busy playing to worry about the movement or the fingerboard."

Guercio brought the band to Southern California in 1967, changed their name to the simpler "Chicago," added a bassist to the sextet, and produced that first double LP for Columbia. The rest is in the books. Three successive top-selling double albums in two years, 200 concerts annually, a European tour that was sold out months before the band left, and on and on.

As Chicago's lead singer and only guitarist, Terry Kath is probably the performer most easily identified with the band. Though he doesn't read music, Terry manages to "write" most of the band's charts.

"Actually, I just tell the guys what I want—or maybe I'll play the different parts—and they just pick it up from there," he says.

Allied Electronics of Chicago made Terry's 60-watt Knight amp. It has two speakers to get the sound he wants without being too loud. Terry says that the Acoustic Control people heard his amp, dug it, and designed the 150 series after it. Today, Terry shares amp duties between the Knight and an Acoustic, depending on the sound of the auditorium they are playing.

Terry has acquired 14 guitars over the past few years, but it is a Fender Stratocaster and a Gibson Les Paul Professional that he uses regularly. On the band's first LP, Terry played a Gibson SG double cutaway.

"The Stratocaster has the best vibrato, but I have trouble bending the strings without slipping off," he says. "My hands are pretty strong—I guess from playing bass all those years."

Anyone who has seen Chicago, has to admire the speed with which Terry plays, It's all natural. No special techniques, no exercises. Normally, he anchors his little finger to the guitar just below the strings. But when he's building one of those incredible solos, or rocking the entire band with an intensely strong rhythmic pattern, he just hammers away with his entire forearm.

"I'm too busy playing to worry about the movement or the fingerboard," he muses. "I just listen to it as it's all happening."

Because of time—and maybe because he's playing so much—Terry doesn't practice guitar.

"I wish I did practice more," he says half-heartedly. "But, mostly, I play the jobs or when I'm working on a tune. Usually in my spare time, I sit around and play drums."

Chicago's first album was produced in a week, Terry sometimes playing a Stratocaster whose neck was held together with a radiator hose clamp. But, generally, a good deal of time is spent on the albums. Keep in mind that not many bands, particularly ones utilizing tight arrangements and a horn section, can produce six excellent records in two years.

The future looks pretty good for Terry Kath, ex-Dick Clarker, ex-Missing Link, ex-Big Thing. Commercially, Chicago can do no wrong. They sell out Carnegie Hall for a week, play before 20,000 at a time, and see their albums sell a million-dollars worth almost before they are released. And, artistically, even the critics who once mistakenly called Chicago "another Blood, Sweat and Tears" are realizing just how wrong they were, and just how creative and adventuresome this young band really is. —*Excerpted from the August 1971 issue of* Guitar Player

Mike Keneally

BY BARRY CLEVELAND | JANUARY 2005

THE STORY OF HOW MIKE KENEALLY PERSUADED THE LATE
Frank Zappa to offer him a gig is legendary. After discovering that Zappa was
rehearsing a new band, Keneally left a message with the maestro's assistant saying that he was "highly conversant with the repertoire" and would like to audition. When an incredulous Zappa called the following day asking whether it was
true that Keneally knew all of his songs, the guitarist replied that he was familiar with them all, prompting Zappa to exclaim, "Well, get your ass down here
and prove it." After a grueling audition, Keneally succeeded Steve Vai as Zappa's
latest "stunt guitarist."

Keneally toured and recorded with Zappa throughout most of 1987 and 1988,
and in 1991, he headed up the Grammy-winning Zappa's *Universe* orchestral performance, as well as beginning a regular association with Dweezil Zappa's band, Z.
The following year, Keneally released his debut solo album, *Hat*, which served as a
springboard for his signature blend of XTC-like pop sensibilities and Zappa-esque
explorations—all buoyed by his often humorous lyrics and virtuosic guitar playing.

During the mid- and late '90s, Keneally performed and recorded with his band
Beer for Dolphins, toured with Steve Vai, collaborated on *The Mistakes* (with Henry
Kaiser, Andy West, and Prairie Prince) and numerous other projects, released a collection of 35 self-performed and produced tracks called *Nonkertomph*, and still managed to write 11 eclectic columns for *Guitar Player*.

The new millennium brought further expansion. Among other things, Beer for Dolphins grew to an eight-piece and recorded the critically acclaimed *Dancing*, Keneally went unplugged with Wooden Smoke, and there were Asian and European tours with Vai. The Keneally juggernaut continued unabated in 2004 with the nearly simultaneous release of the Mike Keneally Band's pop-oriented *Dog* and an ambitious orchestral work, *The Universe Will Provide*, recorded with Holland's Metropole Orkest.

Dog was recorded with your new quartet. What's different about this band and this album?

Dog is the first album I've done with a band that had been working and touring together and had already developed a cohesive sound. It's also the smallest band I've had for a while. We began playing this material in 2001 and started recording it in late 2002. But due to everyone's hectic schedules, we didn't finish the album until early 2004. Because *Dog* took a long time to make—and I had so much time to think about it—it's more polished and finely honed than my other albums. It's also more vocal and song oriented than my other records. There's only one short instrumental, stuff stays in 4/4 longer, and there's very little improvisation.

"The fun begins once you can feel odd times and not have to be intellectual about them."

What is second guitarist Rick Musallam's contribution?

Rick provides a lot of the otherworldly noises that I am less inclined to make. As I continue developing a style that's a more accurate representation of what I'm feeling, I'm becoming less interested in effects and more excited about having a very direct guitar sound. Rick has this huge pedalboard, and he provides a nice contrast to what is now my relatively unaffected tone. As a player, Rick's touch and tone are beautiful and heartfelt—more of a flowing, Scofield-type vibe—whereas my style is a little more angular. So our tones and our approaches mesh well together. He also plays all of the slide guitar parts on the album, as well as bouzouki on a couple of tracks.

You've also released an orchestral record, *The Universe Will Provide*. How did that come about?

Co de Kloet is a producer and on-air talent for NPR in the Netherlands. He was a friend of Frank Zappa's, and he did a lot of radio projects with him. For the last few years, he has been proposing projects that would take me out of my context of bandleader and rock-guitar guy, and that culminated in this orchestral commission. Co really wanted me to work with the Metropole Orkest, because they had played some Zappa material previously, and he knew they could handle difficult material.

You say in your press materials that the music is mostly about your childhood.

Yeah—if the music sounded naïve, I could fall back on that [laughs]. Actually, to keep the composing from being too daunting, I thought back to my childhood—which was really secure and happy, with everything taken care of. The year 1969 kept flashing in my head, so I went back to my eighth birthday with the idea of giving myself this orchestra to do with as I willed. I wanted to create something that would appeal to the kid in everyone.

Describe your compositional process for the orchestra.

Generally, I would transcribe whatever melodies I was hearing in my head by hand, and then Chris Opperman would type them into Finale notational software. If I heard a specific instrument playing a part, I would indicate that on paper. But I'd often just hear the music, and then we'd orchestrate the piece using samples. The other two ways I composed were by clicking notes directly into the computer, and by playing the parts with a MIDI keyboard. The orchestration was a collaborative process. I generally knew what I wanted, but Chris took more of a lead role in some sections.

Are there references to other music, or am I just imagining things?

Some of that happens subconsciously. For example, I didn't realize the opening movement quotes "Happy Birthday to You"—although it's rhythmically displaced. Once someone pointed that out, it was so bloody obvious that I couldn't believe I'd never heard it before. But as one of the guiding concepts was that the music was a birthday gift to my eight-year-old self, I accepted that as a more-than-appropriate intro to the piece—even though it was an accident.

To what extent was the orchestral music improvised?

A lot. There are moments where there's full improvisation from the guitar and moments where there's full improvisation from the orchestra, as well. Initially, I wanted the guitar part to be sort of a floating commentary—not unlike what Miles Davis did on those Gil Evans projects where the orchestra had this set thing, and the trumpet sometimes joined in, and sometimes became this otherworldly voice. But, because there were so many other details to work out, I never quite got the guitar to do that.

What's going on with your modified Stratocaster?

It's one of the earliest Eric Clapton models from 1988. I replaced the Lace pickups with EMG SAs and installed Steinberger tuners, a 2TEK bridge, and a Rich Lewis holographic pickguard. It has been my main guitar for 16 years.

Does it still have the push/pull gain-boost knob?

Yeah, I'm always reaching for that thing. I also knock the pickup selector back and forth a lot, and I go between playing with a pick and with my fingers. I use the volume knob to change the tone, as well as for volume swells. And the treble knob is pretty responsive, so I can get wah-wah effects by turning it while hammering on.

So all of those really huge, ultra-saturated distortion tones are coming from the Strat?

It's a combination of the boost on the guitar and the dirty channel on my Rivera amp kicked into full gain. Occasionally, I'll also add a Boss HyperMetal pedal and/ or a Tube Screamer. That sound can get a little out of control sometimes, but, at moments like that, I'm emulating Coltrane as much as any guitar player. I just want that thick, absolutely commanding tone, where all I have to do is think about a note and it comes out.

Tell me about the Guitarp, which you used on *Dog*.

The Guitarp was designed by Phil DeGruy. Basically, it's a 7-string guitar, but it also has about 14 harp strings. Phil is an amazingly gifted guy, and he plays it in a very sophisticated and beautiful way. I make a much more dunderheaded use of the thing! On "Louie," the 7-string is tuned to what is basically an *A9* chord, and the harp strings are tuned to this kind of weird, sick-sounding melody that I play in unison with Rick. It's just this really strange texture that pops out of the mix. It's great to be able to play with the low A and also have these other strings—which, the way I had them tuned, sounded like bed springs.

Do you use alternative tunings frequently?

The majority of my music is written and played in standard tuning, but every album has at least one song in some kind of altered tuning. It's always exciting to discover what kind of chords come flowing out unexpectedly when you twist a few tuners and see what you end up with.

You play very gracefully over odd time signatures. Do you have any advice for players seeking to do the same thing?

Take it slow at first. Put together a couple of grooves in 5 or 7, and once you get used to how they feel, try soloing over them. The fun begins once you can feel odd times and not have to be intellectual about them. If you have to count during a solo, you won't be able to fully enter the stream of consciousness.

You joined Robert Fripp onstage while on the '97 *G3* tour. How was that?

He was—and is—a really inspiring figure to me. He is someone who is uncompromising in his vision, and he really sticks to it. He'd begin playing when the doors opened, and I thought it was beautiful the way he created these orchestral textures spontaneously. He noticed that I was listening every night, and one evening he gestured for me to come up onstage. I didn't have my stuff set up, so I couldn't play with him that time, but I made sure I was ready the next night! I dealt with the process the same way I deal with any improvisation—I allow the moment to dictate what to do, and I try not to intellectualize too much. And Fripp would provide occasional verbal clues. If he was going to get tonal, he might look over and say, "*C minor, Mr. Keneally*." And then to transition out of that, he might say, "Chromatic hell," which meant anything goes.

Anytime I'm feeling frustrated with the fact I've been playing music this long while selling relatively few records, I realize that's a measure of extreme ingratitude. Because any life that can put me onstage with Robert Fripp is a life that I need to be grateful for.

Kaki King

BY JUDE GOLD | JUNE 2003

"I GUESS MY DAD WAS HIPPER THAN MOST," SAYS KAKI

King. "Instead of sending me off to piano lessons with all the other kids, he forced me to play guitar—and I hated it. I took a few lessons and quit. But my dad always made sure there was a guitar around the house that was small enough for me to play, so I'd pick it up now and then and strum a few chords or check out a Beatles songbook. Then, when Nirvana broke big, it seemed like every boy in my sixth-grade class started to play guitar. All of the sudden, it was cool to be playing, and I already knew way more than the boys did."

Today, King still knows more than a lot of players her age. Fresh out of college, the 23-year-old solo guitarist is making a big noise in acoustic guitar circles with her self-produced debut, *Everybody Loves You*. The buzz began at New York City's Mercury Lounge, where she worked as a waitress and bartender. Scoring some stage time, King won over crowds with intriguing instrumentals that feature hypnotic, jazz-inflected chord progressions, lyrical melodies, and wild techniques such as two-handed tapping and percussive slaps to the guitar body. In addition, she rarely employs standard tuning.

"I like that it's really easy to switch keys in standard tuning," she notes, "but it's hard to play open strings in standard and have them sound glorious. Then again, you can become overly dependent on open tunings. For example, you can be in *DADGAD* and play lovely things forever, but, eventually, it's going to stop sounding interesting. The trick is to keep searching out new tunings and new ideas. One interesting tuning I use is [low to high] *C, G, D, G, A, D*—it gets you away from all those parallel fourths that arise in standard tuning."

Although King was "blown away" after hearing albums by Alex de Grassi and Michael Hedges—and used her ear to learn some of their techniques and tunings— the pivotal moment in the evolution of her style came when she stumbled onto a true mentor.

"I went to the Swannanoa Gathering in North Carolina to immerse myself in guitar for a few days," she says, "and everybody had Martins and Taylors and was playing this lovely sort of Celtic guitar music. It was all very nice, but then I met Preston Reed, and what he was doing was much more interesting than what was going on around him. He tapped riffs, hit his guitar, and, like me, he tuned down a whole-step or more, and was into getting far-out sounds. He even played the exact same guitar as me—an Ovation Adamas. It seemed very serendipitous."

"Banging on the guitar just makes sense to me."

Soon, King adopted some of the techniques used by Reed—such as treating her guitar like a set of bongos while simultaneously playing riffs and chord progressions.

"Banging on the guitar just makes sense to me," she admits. "You have this resonant box that sounds cool when you smack it, so why not go for it? Also, if you're standing onstage for 45 minutes trying to keep people's attention, you're going to have to start screwing around with some interesting ideas."

Another Reed-approved tactic that King uses to wow audiences is tapping melodies on the high frets with her plucking hand while tapping out bass lines and countermelodies with her fretting hand—which is often over the neck.

"It may look wild, but it's really just the most practical way of doing it," she offers. "If I'm tapping something with my fretting hand at, say, the 10th fret, playing over the neck allows my plucking hand to cross over unimpeded and play something down at the 3rd fret or so. And tapping the low strings is a lot easier with your fretting hand over the neck because you don't have to worry about accidentally muting the higher strings. Also, if you're in a tuning such as *DADGAD*, you can very easily tap the lowest two strings with one finger to get instant fifths."

As much as tapping helps King generate musical ideas, it presents a logistical challenge when she plays fingerstyle.

"Long, acrylic nails on your picking hand give you a fantastic plucking tone, but the longer your nails are, the more they interfere with tapping," she says. "Tuning

down helps because the string tension is lowered. This means I don't have to tap straight down. I can tap at an angle so the tips of my fingers still hit the string—even when my acrylic nails are long."

Despite delivering flashy, crowd-pleasing riffs and techniques that sometimes seem like spontaneous combustion, King insists that little or none of what she does is improvised.

"I've never really been one who noodles or takes solos," she admits. "When you're soloing, in a sense, you're improvising a melody, but melodies by themselves really don't mean a whole lot to me. What really gives a melody meaning is how you choose to harmonize it—and that's a lot harder to improvise on the spot. It's not at all arbitrary. For that reason, I hold the compositional aspect of music to be quite sacred. I really value being there during the genesis of a piece and being the person who really felt the song as it was written." —*Excerpted from the June 2003 issue of* Guitar Player

Bill Kirchen

BY ANDY ELLIS | JUNE 2002

THE LAST SEVEN MONTHS HAVE BEEN A WILD RIDE FOR THE
Tele-wielding Bill Kirchen. For starters, he has driven thousands of miles to promote
his new solo album, *Tied to the Wheel*. Then last fall, he and several labelmates formed
the TwangBangers, a six-piece touring outfit that joins Kirchen's dieselbilly rhythm
section—bassist Johnny Castle and drummer Jack O'Dell— with Tele monster Redd
Volkaert, pedal steeler Joe Goldmark, and acoustic guitarist Dallas Wayne. The band's
debut, *26 Days on the Road*, features stunning fretwork from both Volkaert and Kirchen.

Juggling two bands has kept Kirchen busy, but the real surprise came when "Poultry in Motion"—a string-popping extravaganza from *Tied to the Wheel* that pays
homage to James Burton's classic "Corn Pickin'"—received a Grammy nomination
for Best Country Instrumental Performance.

How did it feel to be nominated for a Grammy?
You could have knocked me over with a feather. I fly way under the music-business
radar, so it came as a total surprise. Actually, "Poultry in Motion" was a fluke. I'd
booked some studio time in Texas while I was on the road with my trio, Too Much
Fun. But then I got a killer throat infection and couldn't sing. I'd been goofing around
with this chicken pickin' instrumental idea for a while, so we wrote and tracked it on
the spot. I played my Tele through the studio's blackface Fender Deluxe and used a
Jerry Jones 6-string bass to double that boogie-woogie riff an octave lower.

How do you get those extremely clucky tones?

I use a strange, cross-finger picking technique. It's something I developed in-tuitively, so it took me forever to figure out what I was doing. My thumb plucks a higher string than my index finger—just the opposite of the standard fingerpicking setup. For example, I'll pick the *B* string with my thumb and use my index finger to play the *G* string. Whichever finger isn't plucking dampens the adjacent string, and that's how I get that popping tone.

Since the early '70s, when you played with Commander Cody & His Lost Planet Airmen, you've been known for fast, super-clean riffing. Do you use a locked wrist and straight picking forearm to ensure speed and accuracy?

No, I'm a loose-wrist cat. In fact, I spend a fair amount of time with my pinky planted on the guitar—so much so that I've worn a half-inch trough in my Tele. I plant my finger between the bridge and control plates and wiggle my wrist around from there.

> *"To my ears, the money rig is a Tele through a Deluxe."*

Do you use a heavy pick?

For years and years, I used extra-heavy picks, but I've just switched to Fender mediums. It was a revelation! See, I tend to be ham-fisted. When I played with an extra-heavy pick, the strings would stretch up a damn quarter-tone when I hit them hard. But with a medium flatpick, I don't knock a note out of tune as badly when I attack it. There's also not as much difference between the initial attack and the sustain, and to my ears, that fattens up the tone.

For that quintessential Bakersfield sound—what you hear on old Buck Owens and Merle Haggard records—I use a flatpick and fingers. That's how you get a snappy Tele tone. I think steel players influenced Don Rich and Roy Nichols to pick that way.

What's the secret to getting a good faux steel sound?

You have to let the strings ring against each other. For that, you need an arched hand position, and your amp has to be clean enough to allow each note to be heard distinctly. The idea is to grab notes that work together. You know how Jerry Byrd would play a sixth chord up the neck and work his tone knob for a wah effect? I'll try to ape that by fretting a *D6* at the second position [*F♯, D,* and *B* on the top three strings] and then move that voicing up the neck while waggling either my volume knob or tone knob. It's a tip of the hat to the steel guitar. I'm always trying to nod toward it rather than duplicate it, and I've never tried to do the real intricate bends. I'm interested in the arpeggios and chordal aspects of the steel guitar. My ear is stuck in the major-6th chord—I haven't moved to the major-7th chord yet.

What gear do you use in the studio?

To my ears, the money rig is a Tele through a Deluxe. Someone loaned me a Deluxe back when we were recording the second Cody album, *Hot Licks, Cold Steel &* *Truckers' Favorites.* We cut "Semi Truck" with it, and I've loved that sound ever since.

Your lust for twang has drawn you into orbit with other Tele greats, including the late Danny Gatton. How did you meet him?

I first met Danny in the early '70s, when Al Anderson [NRBQ's legendary Telecaster player] told me there was a guitar repairman in the district. If Al mentioned that Danny was also one of the world's greatest musicians, I sure don't remember it. I took my Tele to Danny to be refretted, and he was extremely personable. He knew who I was—he'd heard *Hot Licks, Cold Steel*—and we sat there talking for a couple of hours while he put new frets in my guitar and made me a brass nut.

He said, "You know, you have an old Tele. You should have round knobs, a round string tree, and a 5-screw pickguard." I'd only owned one Tele—I didn't know from squat. So he gave me all that stuff, and then he said, "Do you want to jam some?" And I remember thinking, "Well, sure. Maybe I'll show this friendly repairman a lick or two." Then—jeez—he started to play. I'd never heard anything like it. To me, Danny had hellacious jazz chops, but he played with a rock and roll sound. None of that "throw your coat over the amp" tone that jazz guys seem to have. He loved Roy Nichols and Scotty Moore, so he had this great combination of snappy tone and reckless, rockabilly attitude.

When I first met Danny, he had a Charlie Christian pickup in the neck position of his Tele. At some point, he and Joe Barden decided it wasn't a good idea to rout out a Tele to put a pickup in it, so they started making a single-blade pickup that would drop into a Tele body. That was the origin of the Barden pickup—which evolved into a narrow, twin-blade humbucker.

I played in a band with Danny for a while. He hired me to be his frontman. I think he enjoyed my sense of humor on the instrument. People would ask me, "Aren't you intimidated by being in a band with Danny?" But I thought it would be pretentious of me to be intimidated by Danny, because there was no way I was competing with him. The way I saw it, I had the best seat in the house.

How do you feel about performing with Redd Volkaert in the TwangBangers?

Performing with Redd reminds me of sharing a stage with Danny. I have to remember to keep playing and not stand there making a trout mouth. To be honest with you, it was so astonishing for me to hear this guy that I had difficulty remembering what it is that I do. It made me focus on my inadequacies, rather than my strengths, and I found myself choking. Not a good place to be when you're performing! But I finally got around it, and in the end, it was educational. I rediscovered a great thing about music: It's not a contest. That's why kids in a garage band who've only played electric guitar for two or three years can make timeless music. There's room for us all. —*Excerpted from the June 2002 issue of* Guitar Player

Dr. Know

BY JOE GORE | JULY 1990

ONE MIGHT CALL DR. KNOW'S BAND, BAD BRAINS, THE greatest American punk group, but if one did, one would be a dork, because that's only part of the story. The Doctor and team have been performing genre-splicing surgery since the quartet was formed in Washington, D.C., 13 years ago, fleshing out their eight-fisted thrashophonic onslaughts with skin sliced from reggae, funk, fusion, and free jazz. Sure, Dr. Know blasts speedcore licks with enough intensity to incinerate most powerchord posers, but he's liable to detour into clean-but-mean linear playing, twisted polytonal excursions, or deep-groove skankulation at the drop of a dreadlock. The fainthearted had better steer clear of Bad Brains' operating theater, because the Doctor is *out*, man.

Bad Brains draw from many styles. What is the common thread?

The message in the music. All our music is about awareness, spirituality, consciousness, and unity. I hate categories. We've been called everything you can call a band like us. An English music paper called us "rasta-punk-oi-thrash-punk-dub." Whoa! Gimme a break! People ask me how I describe our music, and I say "Jah rock." It's rock and roll, and Jah is the influence.

Were you raised with an African consciousness, or did that come to you later in life?

Later in life. Washington, D.C. is a weird place. Since the riots happened, they really try to hold the people down. And since so many people work for the government, they have a false sense of security. They think they're getting somewhere in life because they have this little government job. D.C. is pretty wild. Last year, they had the highest murder rate in America—even though the city is nowhere near as big as New York, L.A., or Chicago. The government has infiltrated a lot of drugs to subdue the people, and that just makes them go off more. It's crazy.

All of us in the band were born and raised there, and we started playing together right after I finished high school. We had a mutual friend who was fortunate enough to have a basement, so that was the jam spot. When his mother would go out to play bingo every Tuesday and Thursday, *that* was jam day. We'd turn up the amps and go crazy. All the local whomevers would come over to his house, and that's how we got to know each other.

Were you playing punk rock from day one?

We were doing a fusion thing for maybe six months before we switched over to punk. Washington is 90 percent black, so all the black music is our roots. The only rock I heard up until '75 or so was some Beatles and Hendrix. That was it. But I got home from work one day, and the guys were playing a Clash or Sex Pistols record. It was a transformation. At first, it was like, "What? You want me to play these three chords and try to sound trashy?" So that's what gave us the inspiration to try to create our own vibe with it. Up until recently, there haven't been many black people playing this kind of music, but these days, black rock guitar players is almost a trend. But all our friends from school supported us, and we just went for it. And we were pretty crazy—dressing pretty wild. So people would just say, "Y'all boys just crazy."

"I really don't like being traditional."

Why did punk speak to you so strongly?

Not necessarily the aggressiveness of it, but the awareness factor. Telling it like it is. The youth these days, we've got to inherit this earth, and we all see what's not happening right. If you don't tell nobody, then nobody will know.

How did you get nicknamed "Dr. Know"?

The "Dr." thing was from a school trip. After I graduated from high school, I went to college. I was in pre-pharmacy, getting good grades. I wanted to go to med school and be a doctor. And I was the one in the band who had the most musical experience when we got together, so that's where the "Know" came from.

One of your early songs was titled "Banned in D.C."

In '77, when punk rock—as they called it in those days—had just been presented in America, we played a concert. At that time, there were only about three places to play in D.C. Everyone would be pogoing, and this one club had a restaurant downstairs. So hearing all the foot-stomping, the people jumping on the floor, and the chandelier bouncing up and down, the club owner was like, "No way!" And this particular club owner knew the other owners, so he called his buddies, and nobody would let us play. They said, "We don't want this music." True of anything different or new, you know? So we started doing concerts in our basement.

Your earliest tunes were modeled after English punk, but you gradually incorporated more original sounds.

That's how it happened. We were able to do that as our musicianship got better, and we figured out what we wanted to do. We purposely tried to put all of our influences in our music—to create our own vibe or whatever. We didn't really have a format, and we still don't. Whatever is happening in our lives at that time is what comes out in the music.

Bad Brains may not have a formula, but you do have distinct musical signatures—such as sudden tempo changes, or the jagged-sounding riffs based on half-steps and tritones.

That was really my trip because I wanted to work in some of the jazz stuff—the "out" stuff. I really don't like being traditional. I hate doing what everybody else is doing, so I go out of my way to do something a little different.

How do you retain the definition on thick chords when you play with so much distortion?

Well, I've been working on my sound for years—basically, because I didn't have any money. But I experiment with different amps, talk to a lot of people, and always try to stay up on the technology side of things. When I first started, there was no technology. It was just get a Super Fuzz, and you're gone [*laughs*]. I have a blown-out Marshall that [New York amp hotrodder] Harry Kolbe did. He's the man. Most of the distortion comes from my amps, but, every once in a while, I use a Boss overdrive pedal. I've been using three Marshalls onstage—one clean, one semi-dirty, and one *killer*.

Your whammy-bar workouts are pretty intense.

I used to pop a lot of strings until I got a Roger Sadowsky guitar. My bar is set up to bend up a half-tone. Sometimes, I rest my hand on the bridge for muting. I used to have tuning problems. I'm not one of those players who would tear up a guitar, but sometimes, I felt like it. But then I got the Sadowsky, and, man, Roger is *it*. It has a Floyd Rose whammy and DiMarzio pickups—two double-stacked single-coils and a double-coil in the back. These days, I use Dean Markley Custom Lights, gauged .009, .011, .015, .026, .036, .046.

I also play a lot of MIDI guitar. I have a Gibson USA-1, which I'm glad I bought because they stopped making it. It has a Photon system pickup that lets me blend the guitar sound and the sampled sound. The Photon unit also has built-in arpeggiation and onboard sequencing and stuff. You can do a lot with it.

I have a Casio sampler—which I like. The system works with the guitar, so it's not like playing keyboards. I use effects like explosions, gunshots, talking parts, and rhythmic things—just to make the music a little fatter. Lately, I've been doing some harmony stuff by having the sampler play along with me. —*Excerpted from the July 1990 issue of* Guitar Player

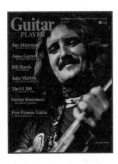

George Kooymans

A PRO'S REPLY | MAY 1975

GEORGE KOOYMANS IS THE LEAD GUITARIST FOR GOLDEN

Earring, a Dutch band that has become quite popular in the United States recently. The following questions were submitted by Jeff Jacobsen of Carlotta, California.

How did you start playing guitar?

We were just playing around with the instrument, Rinus [Golden Earring bassist] and me, and we really were searching and trying to find out what the instrument was all about. We were also trying to form a band. I have never played in a band other than Golden Earring.

When did you actually start playing?

I first played the guitar when I was ten years old, and I am 26 now. My father bought me a guitar because the guys in the streets were getting into rock and roll. I couldn't keep up with them because I was younger than the rest. I tried to keep up by playing rock and roll on the guitar.

Who were you listening to in those days?

I really got off on Eddie Cochran, the Everly Brothers, and Little Richard. The only problem was that I didn't understand English that well, so I had to do everything phonetically. I was just getting off on the sounds.

What was your first guitar?

A Harmony acoustic—which was fine for what we were doing then. My first electric guitar was a Hofner.

What devices do you use with your guitar?

I use an MXR phase shifter, a Gibson echo unit, and a wah-wah pedal. I don't know which kind it is, though.

What kind of guitar do you use onstage?

I use a black, 1958 Gibson Les Paul with three pickups on it. I bought that guitar in Holland. I have a couple of other guitars that I use, too: an old Gibson Firebird, a Fender Stratocaster, an old 12-string guitar, and a very old Gretsch. I also have a Gibson SG Standard that I like a lot and a Fender Telecaster. In the studio, I use all of my guitars.

> *"In the studio,
> I use all of
> my guitars."*

What kind of amplification do you use onstage?

I use a Belgium amp, made by American designers, called a Faylon. I use two Faylon 200-watt slaves and a preamp mixer. For speaker cabinets, I have one bass box with four JBLs in it, a top box with one JBL in it, and a side cabinet that is a Fender box with two JBLs in it.

Have you always used Faylon amps?

No, but recently, yes. I had to replace the speakers in the cabinets because the originals were not very good. I really like the Fender Twin Reverb amps, and I recently got some of those Mesa/Boogie amps. Santana is using them now. Not only are they good amplifiers, but they have a good tone range. I have some old Marshall amps, but they're not very good for me now.

Paul Kossoff

BY STEVE ROSEN | JULY 1976

THE LATE PAUL KOSSOFF, BORN IN LONDON, SEPTEMBER

14, 1950, became the unsung guitar great of Free at the age of 18. That short-lived but successful English quartet split in 1973, with lead singer Paul Rodgers forming Bad Company and Kossoff emerging with Back Street Crawler.

Throughout his career, Kossoff was hampered by poor health and drug addiction and spent much of his time in and out of hospitals. In August 1975, Paul suffered a major heart attack and respiratory failure. A reported recurrence of this condition brought about his death on March 19, 1976, while sleeping on a flight from Los Angeles to New York.

When did you first start playing guitar?

When I was nine, and I heard some Shadows music on the radio. My parents thought I should take lessons, so I had classical training for six years. After that, I sort of got away from playing, and the first real inspiration I had to get back into it was seeing Eric Clapton with John Mayall at a small club. I didn't know who he was or what had gone down, but here's all these people yelling, "God! God!" He really caught my attention, and then I wanted to play. I found that my classical training had no bearing on that sort of music—other than dexterity. After Clapton, my interest grew. I went from him to Peter Green, to B. B. King and Freddie King, and then I got into soul—Otis Redding and Ray Charles. Green and Clapton were very dexterous and powerful at the same time. Clapton is everything I'd like to be.

What type of guitar and amplifier were you using when Free first started?

I was using a Les Paul and a real old Marshall top with a homemade 4x12 bottom that my father helped me build. I used this setup for about a year-and-a-half, and then I got a regular Marshall 100-watt stack.

What equipment are you using now?

The equipment has been nicknamed "The Enterprise." It consists of two cabinets—each containing eight Celestion 12s—and two Marshall tops. I think I'm going to lighten the equipment. I think it's too much. The cabinets were made special for me by Marshall and have bass speakers. I've always liked to use them, because I don't like a lot of top end. With bass speakers, you get a nice, round sound without rasp. I'm also using a Les Paul Standard with a sunburst finish. I think it's about a '57. It had its neck broken once—on the last gig with Free. It went up about 20 feet, and came down on its neck. I thought that was it, but I saw a guy in London named Sam Lee who does beautiful work, and he put it back together. It broke at the 5th fret, and he rebuilt everything from there up—including the tuning head. The only other thing I've done to it is put Grover machine heads on.

"When I'm onstage, I'm too excited to fool around with controls and knobs."

What settings do you use on the guitar and amp?

I use mainly the treble pickup and go between 8 and full up on the amp and guitar. It's very simple. The amp is usually full up, and I control the volume from the guitar. Maybe I'm a little bit too limited with my sounds. I'm not sure. I like to play bluesy things on the bass pickup—with Volume on the guitar set to around 4, 5, or 6. The amp is full up, and then you blast into a solo with your treble pickup. You don't play a billion notes, but you play a few goodies, hopefully—like Freddie or B. B.

You were also using a Fender Stratocaster for a while.

Yes—it's on the cover of the *Back Street Crawler* album. It was a white Strat with a maple neck, but the neck was warped. It was beautiful to play—although you couldn't play any big chords on it—but it was really responsive. I also used a Strat with the last setup of Free I was involved in. I don't know what year it was, but it was an old one. I'm not into years and all that. If it sounds good and feels good, I'll use it. Also, there's no tremolo arm on my Stratocasters. I've never used one, because I've never been into it. Any tremolo I use is from the left hand.

Was it hard to develop such a smooth vibrato?

I think my vibrato has taken a long time to sound mature, and it has taken a long time to reach the speed of vibrato that I now have. I trill with my first, middle, and ring fingers and bend chiefly with my small finger. I'll use my index to back up the ring finger when I'm using vibrato.

Is there a similarity between your vibrato technique and Eric Clapton's?

Probably, yes. He did once come up to me and ask, "How the hell do you do that?" And I said, "Oh, you must be joking!" That was the first time Free was in America, and we were doing the Blind Faith tour.

Why did you change from the Stratocaster to the Les Paul?

I never really changed. One guitar meant one thing and the other something else. The Les Paul is very sensible on gigs. It will not let you down tuning-wise or if I treat it roughly. But if you pull back on the neck of the Strat, it's out of tune—particularly that white one I had. It was harmonically out of tune a little anyway, so you had to make adjustments while you were playing.

Your playing seems totally devoid of electronic effects.

Almost. Onstage, I use a phase shifter, and I've used it on albums a few times. When I'm onstage, I'm too excited to fool around with controls and knobs. I find I can get the sound I want from the guitar and amp—providing everything is working right.

What equipment do you use in the studio?

Basically, it's the same as onstage. When I'm overdubbing leads, I like to be loud, so I can get plenty of power. When I'm cutting a track with the other guys, I'll use less wattage, but I'll still get the same sound at a lower volume.

Your solos on record—"All Right Now," for example—are they thought out before-hand or played as the track is being cut?

Well, on "All Right Now," the bass was put down, and then the keyboard, and then the rhythm guitar. It was best if the solo was simple. It wasn't exactly worked out, but at the time, we were thinking more of effect than of virtuosity.

Is that your philosophy on playing guitar?

I like to move people. I don't like to show off. I like to make sounds as I remember sounds that move me. My style is still very primitive, but at the same time, it has developed in its own sense. I do my best to express myself and move people at the same time.

Do you use any special tunings on electric or acoustic?

No, but I use a lot of open strings, and the chords are neither major nor minor. I don't like to play a major chord unless it's necessary. I prefer to use a chord that rings and that has neither major nor minor dominance. For example, if I was playing a G, I'd press down a D on the fifth string, a G on the fourth string, leave the third string open, get a D on the second string, and a G on the first. That shape can be moved up to a C [8th fret], and a D [10th fret], and an F [13th fret]. There's also a figure I use in A with my little finger playing an A on the bottom E string, while the

A fifth string is ringing open, and I'm getting an *E* on the fourth string, and an *A* on the third string. [*Editor's Note: These chords are characterized by the lack of a natural or a flatted third, which would identify the chord as either major or minor.*]

Are there certain scales you work from?

No. My playing is very primitive. I work from a few chord shapes, but it's really pretty basic. I've never been able to get into the quick runs—the super-duper stuff that Alvin Lee or Rory Gallagher do. It has never really interested me. I do practice whenever I can. With Free, we worked so much there was only time for women and sleep.

What's still in store for your playing?

I think there's still more room to develop. My vibrato is finally starting to grow up. Playing with Paul Rodgers helped me grow. He was my best teacher as to how to enhance a voice, blues-wise. I hate to play just solos. I prefer to hear his voice and back it up, or rip it around, or push it—all without covering it over. My style and his grew up together. —*Excerpted from the July 1976 issue of* Guitar Player

Lonnie Mack

BY DAN FORTE | MARCH 1978

LONNIE MACK IS A BURLY MAN WHO LOOKS MORE LIKE A
lumberjack than a musician. His brooding demeanor and not-quite Southern accent
testify to his rural upbringing. Born Lonnie McIntosh in Harrison, Indiana, in 1941,
his early musical influences consisted mainly of family members and various char-
acters who lived and played socially in nearby Aurora, where Lonnie was raised. He
didn't grow up with his ear pressed to a hi-fi, guitar in hand, because, as he explains,
"Didn't have a record player or nothing. Most of the places we lived didn't have any
electricity, so that made it rather difficult. We were pretty poor."

Later on, Lonnie did acquire an old radio, which exposed him to black music.

"I found this one black station, and that was me," he smiles. "Listened to that
gospel music on Sundays, you know. We lived out pretty far in the country, and my
old man never did drive a car, so we never went anyplace. The radio was it."

When the radio wasn't on, the music played and sung around the McIntosh home
was "country and western and country gospel," says Mack. "We used to have a
whole lot of jam sessions with the family in the old days. My Uncle Bill played the
fiddle, and just about all the relatives on my mother's side were musicians. Sizemore
was their name. My dad plays banjo, and mom does, too. She taught me my first
chords on guitar when I was about five or six."

Lonnie's musical growth was also furthered by hanging out at the hobo jungle
outside Aurora, playing for tips.

"It used to be sort of a meeting place," he recounts. "There used to be a lot of those, but there aren't anymore. There were a lot of neat people there. They liked mostly country music, but I was usually the only musician, except for maybe a harmonica player. We'd play a little blues or something. My dad and my uncle, Harry Dawes, were also into blues, and my dad would take me to see this old colored fellow in Muncie, Indiana, who played the old blues style."

The first musician Lonnie played with in public was also an older black man, a blind singer and guitarist named Ralph Trotto. The apprentice describes Trotto as "a great guitar player. He almost knows too much—one of those kind. He was into a lot of chords, and he taught me to play all the jazz standards. I used to play hooky every day and meet him on the corner on the way to school and hang out and play music. We played for tips at the Nieman Hotel in Aurora."

"Country is never gonna die, and neither is the blues, and rock and roll is kind of a little bit of both."

The first band Lonnie put together, which played mainly rockabilly, consisted of himself and his cousin Harold Sizemore on guitars and a drummer named Rodney Jones.

"We played mostly country songs like 'Oh Lonesome Me,'" he remembers. "We'd just load our stuff in the trunk of the car and drive to different bars and go in and play for tips."

Around this time, Lonnie's mixed musical background—owing to white country, black blues, and gospel music from both sides—began to coalesce into the style that has been his trademark to date. And though his first LP, released in '63, was possibly one of the most successful blends of black and white styles since the early Sun recordings of Elvis Presley and Jerry Lee Lewis, Lonnie claims that "everybody around Cincinnati was doing it. That was what everybody seemed to want to play, you know.

"I think country and blues are about the closest musics there are. They're the earth musics of the white and the black people. Country is never gonna die, and neither is the blues, and rock and roll is kind of a little bit of both."

The guitar style he forged out of this meld, while showing strong ties to his dual heritage, resulted in a sound that was, and continues to be, distinctively Lonnie Mack.

"I think it was pretty much my own way," he feels, "just fooling around with it, stretching and feeling it out, so it would sound good. I'm sure I was influenced by other things, but I'm not exactly sure what. Some of them are just in me, and they come out a certain way."

Lonnie's shift from local following to *Billboard's* number-five spot in 1963 came almost by accident. His band, the Twilighters, was hired to back a group of black female singers called the Charmaines on a recording session for Fraternity Records in Cincinnati. At the session's end, Lonnie and the band laid down two tracks in 20 minutes—one being the now-famous instrumental interpretation of "Memphis."

Several subsequent 45s were released on the small Cincinnati-based label, but with the Duane Eddy/Ventures era not quite over, and the surf instrumental craze just beginning, it was usually Lonnie's powerful instrumentals—including "Wham," "Chicken Pickin'," "Lonnie on the Move," and "Honky Tonk '65"—that got airplay.

Throughout the years, Mack's trademark setup has been his Gibson Flying V played through a Magnatone amp. He bought the V in 1958, the model's first year of production, because, in his words, "it was weird looking. I'd played some Fenders. I bought a Stratocaster when they first came out, and I had some Broadcasters and Telecasters. Then I got a Les Paul and liked it real well. When the V came out, it played pretty much like a Les Paul, and with that shape, I said, 'That's for me.'"

Mack got hooked on Magnatone amplifiers from a Dayton, Ohio, guitarist named Robert Wood, who later went on to form the Ohio Players.

"They're great little amps," declares Lonnie. "The one I had when I cut 'Memphis' was a 460 model with two 12s. The one I have now is a 440 with one 12. They have built-in phase shifters—that's what I like about them. With the Magnatone you've got to turn everything up, and it's still bassy as hell. Usually, I don't turn anything on but midrange, and I run it through a Fender Twin. On the guitar, I play on the bridge pickup with everything full up."

In the late '60s, Lonnie enjoyed a resurgence in popularity, began playing the Fillmore dance/concert circuit, and was signed to Elektra Records. By this time, young rockers who had cut their teeth learning to play Lonnie's version of "Memphis" note-for-note were prospering from their own hits, and Mack, still in his late twenties at the time, found himself in the position of one of rock guitar's elder statesmen. Eric Clapton, Jimi Hendrix, Elvin Bishop, Johnny Winter, and numerous others all took their shots jamming with the mentor, but the combination that Lonnie remembers best was when he was able to back one of his heroes, the late Jimmy Reed.

"I got to play with him in Atlanta, Georgia," he recalls. "It was great. He was drunk in a bar somewhere, and they couldn't find him. I tuned his guitar for him, and he could hardly stand it. It was probably the first time it had ever been in tune. He untuned it right away." —*Excerpted from the March 1978 issue of* Guitar Player

Magic Sam

BY JAS OBRECHT | APRIL 1998

DURING THE MID-'50S, SEVERAL YOUNG BLUES GUITARISTS

on Chicago's West Side forged a tough new sound. Their vocals were moaning and cathartic, their guitar attacks visceral yet melodic. They tended to play with wide, quick vibrato and a piercing sound, and worked easy grooves into exhilarating big-city blues. Leading the pack were Cobra recording artists Otis Rush, Buddy Guy, and the man who seemed to have the biggest crossover appeal of all, Magic Sam. But, while Rush and Guy went on to become top-echelon modern bluesmen, Magic Sam perished in his prime.

Born on Valentine's Day, 1937, as Samuel Gene Maghett, Magic Sam was raised by sharecroppers near Grenada, Mississippi. Relatives revered him as a "music child" as he easily made the progression from diddley bow to harmonica, guitar, bass, piano, and drums. At 13, he moved with his family to Chicago, where he immersed himself in the records of Muddy Waters and Little Walter. By 1955, he was playing in bars with harmonica ace Shakey Jake, who encouraged him to sing. Magic Sam's skillful playing and easygoing personality attracted the friendship of other musicians, including Rush and Guy.

"Sam was just an all-around great guy," Rush remembers. "He was a good-time dude, and he had a lot of fun. Sam wasn't quiet—he was just lively! He might walk up and say, 'President, you got a bug on your head!' That's the kind of guy he were."

"We were the best of friends," adds Guy. "During the '50s, we used to have those

Sunday afternoon guitar battles in blues clubs, where the guy would have a bottle of whiskey out there for the winner. Luther Allison, myself, Otis Rush, Magic Sam, Earl Hooker—we was all doin' that stuff. There was just a lot of clubs back then, and we were playing them in circles. Sam was here on Tuesday, Buddy Guy on Wednesday, Otis on Thursday. It was like that, and it was a lot of fun."

Many of these young players favored Fender solidbodies—in Magic Sam's case, a Telecaster followed by a Strat. According to Guy, "The Fender was Otis, Magic Sam, Freddie King, and myself's type of guitar compared to what Muddy and Son House and the rest of those guys played with—which was acoustics. A lot of them had put the pickup on their acoustic guitar."

"I'm the modern type of bluesman."

Later on, Magic Sam also played semi-hollowbody Epiphones. He often used house amps, and it's likely he had a Fender Bassman. Unlike his peers, he dialed in plenty of distortion and tremolo. ("Sam liked gimmicks," Rush observes.) Playing bare-fingered, Magic Sam would occasionally lick his picking fingers, explaining that this helped him "change the sound."

Rush was the first of the young West Siders to break through, with his heartrending 1956 recordings of "I Can't Quit You Baby," "My Love Will Never Die," and other singles for the Cobra label. On Rush's recommendation, 20-year-old Magic Sam made his recording debut in 1957, cutting with pianist Little Brother Montgomery, upright bassist Willie Dixon, drummer Billie Stepney, and electric bassist Mack Thompson. His first single, an original called "All Your Love," had it all—passionate, vibrato-laden vocals; a sexy, tremolo-washed groove; and an unforgettable solo. Cut at the same session, his "Love Me with a Feeling" romped toward rock and roll, while "Everything Gonna Be Alright" was swamped with enough amp tremolo to make it a prototype of psychedelia (it's likely he used a Fender Tremolux or Vibrolux amp at the session). The following year, Magic Sam repackaged the same riff as "Easy Baby."

With his regular gigs, popular singles, and frequent appearances on ghetto radio shows, Magic Sam hoped to jump to a bigger label in 1959. Then an induction notice arrived.

"Uncle Sam's jive army took him away and ruined his career," former bandmate Syl Johnson claimed in *Living Blues* magazine. "He didn't want to go, so he ran away. He deserted the army, you know. They put him in jail for six months, and he came back, and he hid for a while, and then he wasn't Magic Sam anymore. Not like he used to be."

Eventually, Sam recorded 45s for Chief and Crash and returned to playing clubs, where his extroverted personality and big blues and jazz repertoire made him a favorite.

A decade after his first Cobra recordings, Magic Sam cut *West Side Soul*—one of the defining Chicago blues albums. If anything, his 1967 remake of "All Your Love" surpassed the original. Sam's Mississippi upbringing echoed in the chugging Delta boogies "I Feel So Good" and "Lookin' Good" and the Robert Johnson turnarounds of "Mama, Mama—Talk to Your Daughter." Other tracks were stone big city: "I Need You So Bad," with its cackling leads, and the fearsomely aggressive "Come into My Arms," which carved a path followed by Stevie Ray Vaughan and many others. Sam even cut a memorable "Sweet Home Chicago," using his fingers to simulate a slide. Not a bad two days' work.

With the blues boom in full swing, the album had natural crossover potential, and it received raves in the rock press. Janis Joplin, John Mayall, and others praised his genius, and, for a moment, Magic Sam seemed destined to be Chicago's brightest new blues star. Interviewers found him to be a warm, happy-go-lucky guy with a big smile and a love of barbecue. (He was fond of saying he was a spare ribs cook first and bluesman second.) He was proud of his repertoire, explaining to *Living Blues*, "I am a bluesman, but not the dated blues—the modern type of blues. I'm the modern type of bluesman. But I can play the regular stuff, and also I am a variety guy. I can play the soul stuff, too."

In November '69, Delmark released Magic Sam's second album, *Black Magic*, which he described as "the best album I've heard—and I'm not sayin' it just because it's mine." But by then, years of hard living had taken their toll.

"He was a drinker—no need of me lying," sighs Rush. "I drinked, too, but he was really on it. He don't know when to go home. No sleep, then you gotta work the next night. He'd go take a nap over in the corner, then get up and go play, nap, then get ready and go out again before he go home. That's the wear and tear. That'll get you."

Earlier that year, Sam had collapsed on tour and was hospitalized with a suspected coronary. A stressful California tour soon afterwards further eroded his health. He spent the last few days of his life at home in bed, clutching his guitar. On December 1, 1969, 32-year-old Magic Sam suffered a fatal heart attack. —*Excerpted from the April 1998 issue of* Guitar Player

Mick Murphy

BY MICHAEL MOLENDA | DECEMBER 2003

"MOST MAINSTREAM GUITAR MUSIC SIMPLY ISN'T VERY inspiring," says My Ruin's Mick Murphy, who somehow found the juice to become one of today's most electrifying rock players. "The people who really let go and express themselves outside of a chunk part or a heavy riff are usually in underground bands."

But the only things keeping My Ruin in the "underground" class are the band's underdogs-who-want-to-rule-the-world attitude (a good thing), the vocals of ultra-charismatic frontwoman Tairrie B. (yeah, they're of the shredded-throat, huffed-up Cookie Monster style), and the sad fact the group isn't all over mass-market radio and MTV. The music itself is a thrilling mélange of all the dearest, heaviest, and stunningly rifferific guitar stylings of classic heavy metal, hard rock, thrash, and punk. In fact, if you dig your guitars heavy-in-the-old-school-sense, I can't imagine your listening to *The Horror of Beauty* without goosebumps leapfrogging all over your spine and a clenched fist pumping skyward.

And if you simply can't handle Ms. B's vocals, seek out Murphy and beg him for a copy of his self-produced Neanderthal CD, *Start a Fire with Rock*. Recorded at home on a Fostex MR8 deck with an Alesis SR-16 drum machine, the instrumental project is a jaw-dropping collection of supersonic solos, colossal rhythm punctuations, and fat-ass licks. Trust me, if you name-check Murphy to your buddies, you'll get all the cheese you deserve for turning them on to an emerging guitar hero before he ends up all overexposed and cruising with the champagne-and-limo set. I warned ya.

There's a huge leap in intensity between My Ruin's 2001 album, *A Prayer Under Pressure of Violent Anguish*, and this one. On *The Horror of Beauty*, the riffs seem more thought out and the playing is absolutely go-for-the-throat. What happened?

Well, when I got into My Ruin in 2000, I had just met Tairrie, who needed to start a new band after splitting from Tura Satana. So a lot of the songs on *Prayer* were written, learned, and recorded in a very short amount of time. And remember, I was just in the band—I didn't want to come in and be like, "Hey, it's the 'Lead Guitar Show.'" As a result, I kind of held back a little bit on letting everything loose. But over time, the band evolved, and I started throwing more stuff in and pushing things further and further. I think the new record is way more of an expression of what I do on guitar.

There's also a ton of cool little bits where something very familiar pops up, but it'll be twisted a tad.

I'm definitely aware of my influences, but it's a strange mix. Randy Rhoads is the reason I started playing guitar, but at the same time, Black Flag is a big influence, as well. It's kind of a trip. In the '70s, at a young age, I was listening to stuff like UFO, Deep Purple, Judas Priest, Kiss, and Van Halen. But I'm also into the Ramones and the stuff from the '90s underground scene, like Fu Manchu, Zeke, Clutch, Cathedral, Entombed, and Sleep.

There are also some current underground acts that have some cool guitar—Haunted, Mastodon, Shadows Fall, and High on Fire. Our label, Century Media, has actually opened my eyes to a bunch of European bands that are really heavy. There's definitely a lot of guitar happening over there—a lot of Swedish bands with some crazy guitar—that doesn't get on the American radar. And I should mention that when Megadeth put out *Peace Sells . . . But Who's Buying?*, it became a huge inspiration.

Why that record in particular?

It was a raw album, but it sounded really good. Dave Mustaine and Chris Poland were a very cool, twin heavy metal guitar team—they had two distinctly different styles and sounds that complemented each other really well—and the songs shred.

So how do you scramble in all these disparate influences and cook up a style that's yours?

I think it's just that I have an eclectic mix of influences and I'm self-taught. I've never been into reading tablature or music. It has always been more of a listening thing for me. I totally play by ear. I mean, I learned the basics—scales, chords, and other people's songs—but then I started writing and recording songs, rather than

piecing a bunch of ripped-of riffs together. I think when you start writing, it all goes beyond the guitar, and you start doing things that make sense as a "work."

Speaking of that, there's a real synergy between the guitar and bass on the new record. Sometimes your parts almost sound like one gargantuan guitar. Is that something you guys worked out in advance?

Everything was worked out, but it developed over time. I think the cool part about the new record is that we had a chance to play the songs as a band before we recorded them. We went on tour last year, and half the set list was new songs, so everyone developed their licks in front of an audience. Then we recorded it all really fast. We didn't second guess ourselves in the studio, so the tracks stayed pretty raw.

"The people who really let go and express themselves outside of a chunk part or a heavy riff are usually in underground bands."

How did you construct your tones?

It varies. If we're going to do a droning, slower type of song, I'll go for a "fuzzbox" tone—something with more low end that kind of hums. But if we're doing something that's faster and a little more crazy, I'll go for a sharp, midrange tone with a lot of harmonics. And then there are the vintage distortion tones I'm really into.

I set up overdrives on my Korg AX-1000G to capture different moods. There's a lot of different drives on the record. I basically use the Marshall head for power and that Marshall sound, and I put all the effects in front of it. I've completely customized the patches on the AX. That's something I like to do, and I've spent a lot of time creating different sounds with it.

Besides the AX-1000G, what else is in your rig?

My main guitars are a '71 Gibson Les Paul Standard and a '70s Gibson RD Artist. I run two Marshall 50-watt JCM800 half-stacks in stereo through the AX, and my other main effect is a Dunlop CryBaby 535Q wah. My strings are Ernie Ball, gauged .010–.052, and I usually tune to either D, G, C, F, A, D [low to high] or C, G, C, F, A, D.

What was the studio setup?

Four of the songs on the record were done with my friend Nick Raskulinecz, who also produced the last Foo Fighters album. We're ex-bandmates, and I've known him forever. We used Pro Tools, recording the drums first, then adding the bass and the guitars. The rest of the album was produced by me, and those tracks were done a little more raw at a place called the Dead Zone in Hollywood. We still built up the tracks from the drums, but we recorded everything really fast. We didn't add much—and I didn't orchestrate a bunch of different guitar parts—because we wanted the songs to come off like we sound live.

The record definitely doesn't sound as, let's say, "locked to a click track" as some other current rock releases.

Human feel—that goes back to the '70s, too. A lot of those great albums—like the first Sabbath and Led Zeppelin records—are totally raw. You can tell they just went in there and jammed. That's what we wanted to go for, too. We wanted the record to be tight, but also loose and live. We wanted it to breathe—not be digitized and quantized until every note is measured and perfect. That takes the vibe out of it for me, and it's so overdone now. It's like the big "production technique"—make everything so perfect that it doesn't sound heavy anymore.

Bill Nelson

BY MICHAEL MOLENDA | MARCH 2004

SURRENDERING TO THE COMMANDS OF PURE CREATIVE
thought is one of the most frightening actions an artist can take. Few, in fact, even consider manifesting and then releasing such naked revelations, opting instead to refine and refashion a piece until the final work is far removed from the emotion that inspired it.

On the other extreme, you have Bill Nelson—a creator who adores releasing works in progress, demos, one-take recording projects, and other in-the-moment works. And Nelson doesn't just tempt creative fate with his formidable guitar and music-composition skills, he's also an acclaimed painter, multimedia artist, graphic designer, audio producer, video director, writer, and photographer. While it would be inaccurate to declare that Nelson never tweaks and polishes his projects—he's certainly capable of artistic reengineering—it's the initial spark of wonder and emotion that most informs everything he produces.

Here's another inspiring aspect of this postmodern Renaissance man: Write his name into the search engine of the online All Music Guide (allmusic.com) and be prepared to scroll almost endlessly through his credits. Since his emergence as a folky solo artist in 1971, through his late-'70s guitar hero days with Be Bop Deluxe, to his incarnation of the past 20-odd years as an aural adventurer, Nelson has produced a phenomenal amount of music. He is truly someone who has been blessed with an antenna that constantly finds illumination in all things, and he's the perfect artist to open our forum on the mysteries of creativity.

Be Bop Deluxe (left to right): Simon Fox, Bill Nelson, Andrew Clark, and Charles Tumahai

You're extremely prolific. How do you maintain such a high level of inspiration?

There are so many areas that inspiration can come from, and each lesson or discovery can bleed over into my music. These things inspire ways of treating music and ways of thinking about music. Even esoteric studies—such as the occult and the Rosicrucian thing I was into for a long time—have helped me understand the way one's mind works. By understanding that a little bit more, you can better understand the way imagination works, and that there are other possibilities of expressing quite ordinary ideas in unusual ways by looking at them from another angle. It's a matter of freeing yourself from that trap of being on a set of rails going in one direction—the way you're "supposed" to go according to whatever culture you've grown up in. You must have the audacity and nerve to be able to step outside of that and explore what else is there.

So for me, inspiration is not purely from musical areas—or even from the point of view of the guitar. Although in the last few years guitars have suddenly reared their heads again. I've gotten a second wind with the guitar. I listen back to where I started out as a young teenager being excited by the sound of the guitar, and many of my more recent inspirations have been from listening to guitar players who were recording before I was playing. I've been buying albums by Les Paul, Kenny Burrell, and Hank Garland, and a lot of western swing. So I've rediscovered that thing that first kicked me into wanting to play guitar, and it really doesn't have much to do with the '60s stompbox revolution. It's a purer kind of sound. I even bought myself a couple of Gretsches this last year because it's the sound of those guitars particularly that woke me up to what it was that excited me about guitar playing in the first place.

Can you specify how non-guitar influences might influence your musical direction?

Well, I think there are several levels those kinds of things can work on. One level is that if you enjoy literature and visual arts, those things can spark so many ideas for lyrics. And cinema can spark ideas for development and arrangement. The way you can arrange a piece of music is very similar to editing a film and choosing camera angles and lighting. On a technical level, just being excited by the way a camera moves within a story line can inspire the way sound moves or how an instrument moves within a musical arrangement. Those visual cues translate to placing a mic to get a sound at a certain distance because you have an atmosphere that is unique to that particular position or the amount of rever-beration you add to a sound.

Your muse has often moved you away from playing the guitar—instead prompting you to utilize samples, keyboards, and the recording studio as the main tools of your creative ideas.

Well, I tend to be stubborn in that when a lot of people jump on whatever the new bandwagon might be, I tend to jump off and look for another direction. And I did the same with guitars. There was a period in the late '70s and early '80s when the language of electric guitar was written

"I can draw on all these different periods and influences and just let them all mix together quite naturally."

in stone, and it was very difficult to move outside of it without people becoming completely crazed and angered by what you did because they expected a guitar to sound and behave a certain way. And keyboards suddenly presented me with other opportunities.

So part of your approach is avoiding convention?

You have to! For example, my studio is 24-track digital, and I've got all the technology I need. But so does everyone else, and because of that, there's a certain uniform quality coming out from a lot of musicians that makes things less individual. And, at this time, I've found that by going back to some roots things and mixing those in with technology, I can cover a wider range of expression and atmosphere and hopefully come up with something slightly unique.

The issue of individuality is constantly debated by musicians, but I think few of us actually manage to craft something unique.

Perhaps, but every musician still looks for his or her own voice and their own language. Maybe I found that a long time ago—it's difficult to judge from the inside—but I'm starting to hit a point where I look at what I've done and add it all up to see what equation emerges. My palette is broader than it has ever been, and I'm comfortable enough to move—within one piece of music—through lots of different styles and techniques. And there isn't that compartmentalization between one part and another. I can draw on all these different periods and influences and just let them all mix together quite naturally.

Many musicians find it difficult or intimidating to open themselves up to so many creative options.

It's difficult to grasp where my particular impatience comes from. It's an ongoing search for new kicks and new stimulation. What really excites me is when I'm not necessarily operating from a guitarist's template of technique and licks. It's being thrown into a space that needs a different kind of head on the shoulders to explore it, rather than a guitarist's head. First and foremost, it starts from the point of view of art—and I know that's an overblown word—where you think about things as being a creation of some kind. It doesn't matter necessarily that they're musical, just that there's some kind of vision—a dream of something brought into the world that's interesting to me first and hopefully to other people. And then I look at the tools I have in front of me. And some of those tools are guitars, some are keyboards, some are percussion instruments, and some are recording instruments. I've got a video editing setup at home now, so video has become another angle. All of those things can make a whole variety of expressions.

With so many avenues for creation at your disposal, how do you focus your energy into a singular artistic statement?

It's hard at times, because I have a history. What I'm keen to do is keep things fresh, but I'll think to myself, "Well, where do I start?" And you can deliberate forever, but you just have to jump in. For example, I recently did a show where a grand piano was onstage. I hadn't prepared anything for piano, and I hadn't played an acoustic piano for a long time, but I said to the sound guy, "Put two mics on this, and I'll use it somewhere in the set." When I got to a particular point, I improvised two loops with a Boss Loop Station and a Line 6 Delay Modeler, and then I walked over to the piano, sat down, and played. I had no idea where I was going, but I knew something would emerge.

It's like throwing yourself into a lake and holding your breath and waiting for the water to float you to the top. It's a matter of trust. If you think about it too much, you'll never do anything, because you'll always see the downside—you'll think, "Well, that could go wrong, and maybe I'll make a mistake." But if you're a musician, you should trust what you are, because, like the water, your musicianship will lift you up. It will save you.

It's almost a Zen thing: Does a daffodil have to think about being a daffodil? No, it just is. So if you're a musician, after you've put a certain amount of years and practice in, you should have a basic understanding of what your instrument does. At that point, making music is no longer a matter of sitting down and rehearsing chops or anything like that. It's a matter of trusting the instrument and trusting your own instincts with it. And if a mistake happens, then go with it and turn it to your advantage. It's an adventure.

Here's another example: For my latest tour, I had a set of prerecorded tracks, which were obviously fixed, but they were nonlinear arrangements with odd angles. They weren't the easiest things to remember, so there were always points where I was never sure what was going to happen next—no matter how many times I worked with the tracks. And so there were times when I suddenly realized I was falling back on licks from somewhere in my history. Sometimes that was good, because they were signature things, and they became something the audience could recognize. But other times it was bad, because those familiar lines were not where I should have been going. I should have been challenging myself and moving in a different direction. Those evenings when I surprise myself are happy times. The nights when I fall back on the safety net are the times when I'm a bit pissed off with myself.

What types of stimuli tempt you to play it safe?

Basically, it boils down to the minute I start to think about how the audience might react. Then I'm in trouble. The best performances are completely unselfconscious. They're where you're inside the music, and it's leading you, and you just follow where it goes. There's no thinking whether it's right or wrong or if it's entertaining people. That's all out the window. The minute you start to analyze what you're doing, all kinds of doubts creep in, and you lose the music. The music is no longer this organic, living, breathing thing—it's something you try to knock into shape with a set of rules you've picked up over the years.

It's dangerous to think too much. The thinking should be done at an early stage in a musician's career. And then when you get to that stage and just let go, it becomes a blissful experience to play. That's hard to achieve. No matter how many years you've been playing, that moment of being completely one with the music is not so common. It's not something you can guarantee every time, no matter how you approach it. It's the magic—the X-factor—that still makes life interesting for everyone who is listening and everyone who is playing.

Can you consistently put yourself in a place where everything is open and ready to accept the drama of the moment?

Not really. It's not a technique, you see. If it were, then you'd be able to apply it consistently and create magic. I don't know what puts me in the right space—the space where things happen—where I'm surprised and entranced by what's going on, and the thing is playing me, instead of me playing it. Those moments do happen, but how you get there is impossible to plan. All you can do is try to eliminate as much worry and self-criticism as possible.

Also, when you're playing live, the audience is critically important. If you have that rush of energy from them, and they're struggling with you to get something from the music, then that puts you in the right space to deliver something wonderful. It's not a matter of them being passive and saying, "Okay, impress me." They have to put feedback in there, and that feedback can transform the most nervous and unconfident player into someone who is really awesome.

Given all the many mental, emotional, and technical tools at your disposal, what typifies your main engine of expression?

For me, it's the simple joy of playing the way a child plays. When you're a little kid, you don't think intellectually, but you experience tremendous joy playing with building bricks, household objects—whatever you're given to play with. As a child, I remember pouring water from one pan to another for ages; just watching that stream go from one vessel to the other was so beautiful. There's no sort of logical thought process involved other than the simple appreciation of water flowing from one container to the other. And it's that purity—that simplicity—that often gets lost in the mental process of dealing with music. I think if you can approach music with that purity—a belief that everyone has the potential to produce something astonishing—then you can connect with your creativity on a very fundamental, basic, and deep level.

Jimmy Nolen

BY LEE HILDEBRAND
WITH HENRY KAISER | APRIL 1984

"JIMMY NOLEN WAS THE FOUNDER OF FUNK GUITAR," STATES bandleader Johnny Otis, "yet the very people who are influenced by him are not aware of it at all. He was a giant influence in American music."

Nolen, who died of a heart attack at age 49 on December 18, 1983, played on several Otis sessions in the late '50s, including the hit "Willie and the Hand Jive," but developed his pervasive funk style during his 16 years with James Brown. Nolen was more than a stylistic innovator. Until his death, he remained the standard by which all other funk guitarists were measured.

Although he was primarily a rhythm guitarist, the impact Nolen had on subsequent players was no less important or farreaching than the influence of rock/R&B innovators such as Chuck Berry, Jimi Hendrix, and B. B. King. His distinctive style of sixteenth-note strumming, and funky, choppy chord work (relying heavily on 7th and 9th chords) provided the foundation on which virtually all modern R&B, funk, and disco guitar is based.

Nolen's now-trademark rhythm guitar style was introduced to the world in 1965, on James Brown's trend-setting "Papa's Got a Brand New Bag." Nolen remained with Brown until his death, with the exception of a two-year break (1970–72) when virtually the entire Brown band defected and, under saxophonist Maceo Parker's leadership, began performing and recording as Maceo and All the King's Men.

ROSE GARDEN

PISMO BEACH

FRI. AUG. 5 -

9 p.m
till ? ?

JIMMY NOLEN AND BAND

WITH

MARIE ADAMS

AND THE 3 TONS OF JOY

In the following interview, conducted in San Francisco nine months before his death, Nolen talks at length about his one-of-a-kind guitar approach and his long-time association with Soul Brother Number One.

You haven't gotten the recognition that's due you. Does that hurt?

Yeah, it hurts. There are other things I could be into—like recording with differ-ent groups if they really knew who I was. There are so many guitar players who patterned their style off of my style since I joined up with James Brown in '65. My first recording with Brown was "Papa's Got a Brand New Bag," and somehow or another, those licks that I hit in there were ring-ing out, and a lot of guitar players are using them nowadays. One way or the other, they connect it up—a little bit of their style and a little bit of my style.

"So many times, I had to play guitar and drums all at the same time."

I borrowed a few styles from some of the guitar players coming up myself—like Pete Lewis with Johnny Otis and Wayne Bennett [guitar player with Bobby Blue Bland], who was one of my idols. You know, it all started with B. B. King.

You've said that part of the reason you haven't been recognized is that James hasn't put your name on any of the albums.

That's true. Not only my name, but he just don't give none of his musicians credit. I really can't say why.

Did you ever ask him?

I never did. That was one of his policies. I'm only one man. Most of the albums that's being recorded nowadays, you look on the back, and you can see who's playing what.

When you first started playing guitar back in the late '40s, what were some of the sounds that you started to pick up on?

I used to play around with the T-Bone Walker style. Back during the time I was trying to learn, T-Bone was the most popular guitar player there was. He was the first guy I started listening to, and Muddy Waters and all those guys like that.

How did you start with James Brown?

He happened to come to Los Angeles one Christmas, and his guitar player, Les Buie, decided that he wasn't going any further. I was recommended for the job through a friend who was working with James Brown—L. D. Williams. We used to work together.

Did you have to audition?

I didn't have to audition. I just started out, and I went on the stage the first night. It was kind of frightening. His music is very swift—you have to be thinking fast. There's no time for no mistakes up there.

What did he say to you afterwards?

He told me I'd done a great job for the first night.

How did you prepare for the first night? Did you already know the tunes?

I already knew his hit tunes. Of course, there were a lot of in-between tunes that he was doing to make up a concert that I wasn't very familiar with.

How did you make it through the tunes you didn't know?

I'd stand next to the organ player, and he'd fill me in on the changes. It went pretty smooth for the first night. It was kind of frightening. I'll never forget it.

How are James Brown's tunes worked out for recording sessions?

Right there on the spot. Mostly, on all of his hit records, he has thought them up in his mind—as far as lyrics, and a general idea of how he wants his rhythm to go. To put the tune together, it's not written or anything. You just get there, strike a groove, and you go from there.

Onstage, are you always watching and listening to him?

You must be alert with him.

Is it true that he fines musicians for making mistakes?

He used to, but he don't anymore. He used to take the fine money and throw a big party for the whole band. It's good in a sense, because it makes you tighten up on your axe. Like I say, playing with him, there's no room for mistakes, because everything is swift. The key to the whole thing is to watch him. He is more or less like a director, singer, and dancer all in one.

Did you ever get fined?

Yeah. I paid a few. We had a good time, though. He'd throw a big party in New York when we'd have some time off. Nothing but a lot of fun. It made me sharp.

When did you start to develop that fast, sixteenth-note strumming that you're noted for?

I started developing that during the Johnny Otis days. It used to be that with so many different drummers—some of them were good, but some were just lazy—I used to just try to play and keep my rhythm going as much like a drum as I possibly could. So many times, I had to play guitar and drums all at the same time. You know what I mean? By keeping that rhythm going, it kind of keeps the drummer straight. Unless you're playing with a drummer year after year for so many years, it's very hard to get with a drummer and click it off.

"Papa's Got a Brand New Bag" seemed to be a turning point in James' style.

It was the turning point. His previous tunes were more or less a lot of blues and stuff like that. It was either slow or real, real fast. That was the first tune that he ever just dropped back with it and set it in the pocket. He came up with that style of laid-back music, and that started a whole lot of different groups and musicians going in that vein. He started a new trend in music at that time, because the drummers had been either shuffling or playing his style of music.

What type of chords do you play with Brown?

I use a lot of raised 9ths. He has a whole lot of 9ths in his music. As you'll notice, there are not too many chord changes in most of his hit tunes. You lock in on one chord. Most of the musicians are doing that. They lock in on one basic chord, throw in what they call a bridge in between for a few bars, and then fall right back and lock into that groove again. James started that kind of thing, and a lot of musicians are doing it even right now.

What kind of guitar did you play on "Papa's Got a Brand New Bag"?

That was a Gibson ES-175—one of the early-style guitars. T-Bone and Lowell Fulson had them.

What amplifiers do you use?

Mostly Fenders. I've used Peaveys in the past. Right now we're using Fender Twin Reverbs. I put Volume on no more than 6, Treble is on about 8, Bass is about 5, and Midrange is about 6.

Do you get tired of playing the same songs all the time?

I really do, but James has had so many great tunes that it's almost impossible to say you can't play them anymore. —*Excerpted from the April 1984 issue of* Guitar Player

Mary Osborne

BY LEONARD FERRIS | FEBRUARY 1974

MARY OSBORNE HOLDS A UNIQUE PLACE IN GUITAR HISTORY.
She is virtually the only woman guitarist to play a role in jazz. At the age of four, Mary was playing the uke around her Bismarck, North Dakota, home. Her mother and father both played guitar. Mary's father had his own band—a string group—and when she was ten, Mary joined on banjo. She was fascinated by all the string instruments, and at the age of nine, Mary Osborne became a guitarist.

"When I picked up that first guitar," she recalls, "that was it. I knew that's what I wanted to play the rest of my life."

She spent her teens working various Bismarck clubs, singing and playing jazz guitar. At 17, though, her musical life changed almost overnight.

"The only electric guitar I'd heard was the Hawaiian," she says. "But some musicians told me to drop by a place called the Dome to hear this guitarist who was working with the Al Trent sextet. The man was Charlie Christian. It was the most startling thing I had ever heard. I had listened to all the jazz guitarists of the time—Dick McDonough, Eddie Lang, Django—but they all played acoustic. And here was Charlie Christian, playing Django's 'St. Louis Blues' note-for-note, but with an electric guitar. I'll never forget that day."

She and Christian later became friends, but his influence on her music began at that instant. In fact, the next day, Mary scouted the local music stores until she found a Gibson like his. It cost her $85. For another $45, she got a friend to build her an amp.

Shortly afterward, Mary joined the Winifred McDonald Trio, playing dance tunes, some jazz, and a lot of Andrews Sisters things. The group went on the road, playing six months here, six months there, until they landed in St. Louis, where bandleader Buddy Rogers heard them and hired the trio as part of his show.

The band eventually landed in New York and then broke up. Mary's reputation earned her jobs with numerous radio stations and recording companies as a sideman. It was during this time that she won the Esquire Jazz Poll and began sitting in at sessions all along 52nd Street's jazz clubs. It was also during this period that she joined the trio of pianist Mary Lou Williams.

Ralph Scaffidi—a young trumpeter with the Dick Stabile band—met Mary and got her a job with the orchestra. After a period playing together, the two broke up their relationship while she went on the road with Terry Shand, Russ Morgan, Raymond Scott, and Joe Venuti. Ralph joined Tommy Dorsey, then Les Brown, and spent time with the CBS staff orchestra before going in the service.

"When I picked up that first guitar, that was it. I knew that's what I wanted to play the rest of my life."

Mary found herself in Chicago, freelancing to radio stations, jazz clubs, and the like, recording with violinist Stuff Smith under the eye of jazz critic/producer Leonard Feather.

In 1944, Feather brought her to a radio performance in New Orleans—her first concert appearance. The national exposure brought her immediate recognition among jazz fans from one coast to the other. She then moved to Philadelphia.

Here, one day, she heard about a bigname jazz concert to be held at the city's Academy of Music. Showing up backstage to see a few friends, she heard herself being announced as a surprise guest. A guitar was pushed in her hands about the same time she was pushed onstage. She whispered a few titles to the backup band and was on her way.

"The response was great," remembers Mary. "I couldn't believe it. I turned to the band that was backing me, and there stood [tenor saxist] Coleman Hawkins. If I'd known that before, I'd have never been able to play."

Ralph Scaffidi and Mary got married after his discharge from the service and moved back to New York, where she formed the Mary Osborne Trio with Sanford Gold on piano and bassist Frenchy Couette. They opened at one of the more important jazz spots, Kelly's, and ended up staying on for a year. It was here that Django Reinhardt heard her, regularly coming to the club. Everything started breaking for her again—radio shows, more clubs, and a recording contract with Signature.

Later, she brought Jack Pleis on as pianist and signed a new record deal—this time with Decca. But the trio broke up in 1949, and Mary went out on her own, doing some *Arthur Godfrey* TV shows and assorted stage appearances.

From 1952 to 1962, Osborne was one of the busiest musicians in New York City, working the *Jack Sterling Radio Show* on CBS in the morning with the Elliott Lawrence band, then doing the *Ted Steele* TV program in the afternoons. At night, she was recording with people like Mitch Miller and various jazz groups, and cutting her own *Girl and Her Guitar* album with Tommy Flanagan on piano in 1959. And somehow, during all of that, Mary managed to have three children.

In 1962, she began a five-year period of classical guitar study with Alberto Valdez-Blaine. At the same time, she continued playing clubs and began taking on students.

In 1968, she and Ralph moved to Bakersfield, California. There haven't been many record dates since then, but Mary Osborne is as busy as ever. She plays at clinics for her husband's Rosac amplifier company, works four nights a week with her own quartet at the Hilton Hotel, teaches both in the classroom and privately, and is embarking on an entirely new career as a concert guitarist, working both the Newport and Concord festivals among others.

Her guitar is a handmade 1963 Bill Barker model, made in Toledo, and given to her by friends. Mary's amp, naturally enough, is a Rosac. A model 410 with 150 watts and four 10" speakers.

Eddie Phillips

BY BARRY CLEVELAND | MAY 2007

FOR A FEW YEARS DURING THE MID-'60S, THE CREATION
seemed poised for stardom. One of the first guitar-trio-plus-vocalist lineups, the
band toured with the major acts of the day, appeared on mainstream television in
England and Europe, and recorded with legendary producer Shel Talmy. Songs such
as 1966's "Painter Man" and "Biff Bang Pow" wedded catchy vocal hooks to edgy
neo-hard rock while most English bands were still clinging to the red coattails of
the British Invasion. Furthermore, lead guitarist Eddie Phillips routinely slapped,
sawed, and otherwise played his Gibson ES-335 with a violin bow. Why the band
never achieved greater recognition remains a mystery.

There's a persistent rumor that Pete Townshend invited Phillips to join the Who
as a second guitarist, and while there is evidence that Townshend may have considered such a move, he never approached Phillips about it directly.

"I'm not sure how that started, and I don't know if it is true," says Phillips. "If he
had asked, however, I would have turned him down, as the Creation was number
one for me at the time."

The Creation disbanded in 1968, but throughout the intervening years, Phillips
has continued to support himself by writing and playing music. Boney M's 1978
cover of "Painter Man" sold more than seven million copies, and hit versions of
Phillips-penned songs by Rockpile, the Shadows, the Woolpackers, and others have
kept the revenue streams flowing. The Creation re-formed briefly in the '90s, per-

forming at the Royal Albert Hall in 1994, and a version of the band is still active from time to time.

Was your original ES-335 modified in any way?

I removed the chrome pickup covers to improve sustain, and I took off the scratch-plate because it got in the way of the violin bow, but otherwise it was a standard 335 with block inlays. A big plus for this guitar was that it had Little Richard's autograph on the back. I'm a huge fan of his, and we toured with him in 1967. He signed it on the last night of the tour at Leeds Town Hall.

"I tried using a hacksaw with the blade replaced by a .046-gauge guitar string, but that didn't work, so I tried out the bow."

What amps were you using back in the '60s?

I played through two 100-watt Marshalls. At the beginning of 1967, I changed from using four 4x12 cabs to two 8x10 cabs, as I liked the sound of the 10s better. With the Mark Four, which was pre-Creation, I used a Vox AC30, which was good for controlled feedback. An example of this is on "I'm Leaving," recorded around1964.

Did you use any effects?

The only effect I used was a treble booster built for me by an electronics wizard friend named Les Coulson. It was a five-position tone booster—like a graphic equalizer on a switch—built into an Old Holborn tobacco tin.

When did you begin playing with a bow and why?

That was around 1964, and it began with a desire to create sustained notes. I tried using a hacksaw with the blade replaced by a .046-gauge guitar string, but that didn't work, so I tried out the bow. That didn't work at first either, until I realized that I had to rosin it!

Did Jimmy Page steal the idea from you?

Yes!

What sorts of strings did you use in the '60s?

In those days, you couldn't buy custom-gauged strings, so you had to fiddle around with different sets to get what you wanted. The gauges were probably .009, .011, .016, .026, .038, and .048.

What gear are you currently using?

I play an early '80s Fender Stratocaster, a reissue dot-neck Gibson ES-335, a Gretsch White Falcon, and a DeArmond with FilterTron pickups. I use an old MXR Distortion Plus and a Boss EH-2 Enhancer, and everything goes into an old Fender Twin Reverb with Altec Lansing speakers. My strings are Ernie Ball Hybrid Slinkys (.009–.046).

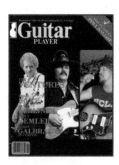

Emily Remler

BY ARNIE BERLE | SEPTEMBER 1981

SELDOM DOES A WOMAN VENTURE INTO WHAT IS GENERALLY considered the man's realm of jazz guitar. Indeed, most people can only name a handful of famous female guitarists in any genre. But at 23 years old, Emily Remler is making inroads not only into jazz guitar (for which she is best known), but also rock, funk, and various fusion styles for studio sessions. Experienced jazz veterans such as Jim Hall, who calls her "just incredible," and Herb Ellis are among her many admirers.

In 1978, at the Tenth Anniversary Concord Summer Jazz Festival in Concord, California, she shared the stage with Ellis, Barney Kessel, Cal Collins, Howard Roberts, Tal Farlow, and Remo Palmier on a venue billed as a "Guitar Explosion." She has performed with the "Great Guitars"—Charlie Byrd and Herb Ellis, substituting for Barney Kessel—and has worked with New Orleans' esteemed jazz clarinetist Pete Fountain.

A native of Englewood Cliffs, New Jersey, Emily started playing folk music at age ten.

"My brothers played guitar," she recalls, "so the instrument was around the house, and I started to teach myself to play. I never really practiced—it was mainly for fun."

A few years of formal lessons left little impression, and her interest shifted from folk to rock. Although little more than a hobby at first, playing guitar took on a more important role as Emily was exposed to music theory at boarding school in her teens.

"It became a challenge. I always liked challenges."

Upon graduation from high school, Emily enrolled at Berklee College of Music in Boston, where she was exposed to the works of jazz guitarists Wes Montgomery, Pat Martino, and Charlie Christian. With her Berklee diploma in hand, she moved to New Orleans and became one of the busiest guitarists in town, playing everything from mainstream jazz to contemporary rock.

"It turned out to be the best move I could have made," she says, "because I got all my experience down there. There weren't too many guitar players around, and I was one of the few who could read, so I got all the show gigs and, later, some jazz and even rhythm and blues gigs."

"The fact that I'm a girl is secondary."

In New Orleans, she met Herb Ellis, who invited her to appear at the Concord festival. A contract with Concord Records soon followed, and the result was Emily's first solo album, *The Firefly*.

Has the fact that you're a woman had either positive or negative effects on your getting work or being taken seriously as a musician?

Both positive *and* negative. There have been times when it seemed to help, and that did bother me, but there was such a long period of *not* getting gigs because I'm a woman that it was simply refreshing to get gigs for any reason. Hopefully, I can overcome that aspect by playing well, and people will forget about it. On records, no one can see me, so if the music's not good, then I won't get hired. But I do agree that it's definitely something of a novelty, and since there is nothing anyone can do about it, I might as well use it to my advantage.

Have people suggested carrying the novelty further, say, by putting together an all-girl band?

Oh, yes, but I have no desire to do that. In fact, the whole women's thing—I'm not interested at all. Many women are angry and trying to make a political statement, and all I want to do is to play my guitar. The fact that I'm a girl is secondary. It's something I'm hit with as soon as I come off the bandstand, but when I'm up there playing, I don't think about what sex I am.

How important is composing to you?

Actually, I think of myself more as a composer than as a guitarist. I want to be a composer more than anything else. Eventually, I'd like to write for movies. But right now I'm into guitar, so I'll make the switch later on.

At Concord's festival you were in some very heavy company—Herb Ellis, Tal Farlow, Barney Kessel, Howard Roberts, and others. Were you nervous?

Well, first of all, the guys are so nice that they make you feel relaxed right away. And don't forget, I had already done a gig with Herb Ellis and Charlie Byrd in the

Great Guitars. Barney Kessel is in that group, but he couldn't make this particular date, so I was asked to take his place. Well, I made sure I knew my part for the festival. When it came time to play there with Herb, I was very prepared so that I wouldn't be nervous.

How did you go about getting ready for such an important gig?

First, I made sure I got there early, so that I could go over the music with all my might. When I worked with the Great Guitars, I bought their records and learned all three parts, because I wasn't sure which one I would have to play. For that job, I was *really* prepared. I'm a great believer in copying things off of records. I've always done it. It's a great way of developing the ears. First, you start off with little bits of solos, and they gradually become whole solos. I've done complete transcriptions like that.

Is your approach to learning jazz different from your approach to rock?

Yes, I have a definite way of looking at jazz. There are two basic scales, the melodic minor and the Lydian. They may be applied in certain ways to get you through a lot of situations. Let's say you have a dominant-seventh chord moving down a fifth. For example, from $G7$ to C in the key of C. You can play the melodic minor scale a half-step higher than the root of the dominant. In this case, the dominant is $G7$, so for that chord you can play the $A\flat$ melodic minor scale. Now, if the dominant chord does *not* resolve to the tonic chord, then you play the melodic minor scale built from the 5th of the dominant. The 5th of G is D, so for a $G7$ that doesn't resolve to C, you play the D minor melodic scale. This D minor is the II of the key, which is a very typical thing—it creates that nice minor-major sound.

Why use the $A\flat$ melodic minor scale for the $G7$ only if it's going to the C chord?

Because it provides all those tension notes, and when it finally resolves to the C [the I chord, or tonic], there is a greater sense of tension release. If you just play on the $G7$ scale and then change to the C, there wouldn't be too much difference. You want that feeling of movement toward the I chord. If the change isn't going to the I, you don't need that tension—there's no demand for the resolution. So with the second alternative of playing the Melodic Minor scale based on the 5th of the dominant, you get that minormajor sound, which is so desirable because of its bluesy feeling.

In light of all your work with singers, can you offer any advice on accompaniment?

The important thing I've learned is that you shouldn't overpower singers—you must complement them. They're carrying the melody, they're on top. Don't let your ego get in the way. Don't whip out all of your guitar licks that you've been practicing. I think I'm a successful accompanist because I'm sensitive. And if sensitivity is a part of your personality, then that's all you need.

Do most singers give you the chords or a lead sheet and leave the rest up to you?

Sure. Most chord sheets for guitar are ridiculous anyway, as are a lot of big-band charts, because of the way they give you every chord that the horns are playing when all you need to play is the basic skeleton of each chord. That's one thing that Herb Ellis taught me. When a dominant seventh chord is given, all you have to play is just the tritone, because the horns are taking care of the chord's upper-structure tension notes. If you play them, too, you'll just get in the way. They need the bottom.

When you were into rock, whose music did you like?

Johnny Winter and Jimi Hendrix. I was crazy about them. I wasn't good enough to play like them—especially Hendrix—because I only played with one finger in those days. How much could I do? But I loved everything they did, and I could sing everything they played note-for-note. That's why I knew I'd become a musician. I could sing the whole solo by Ravi Shankar from the album *Concert for Bangladesh*. I knew the entire raga note-for-note.

Have you been as concerned with equipment as you've been with musical styles?

Well, my first guitar was a Gibson ES-330, and I recently went back to playing on that same instrument. I tried others, but some were too fat and restricted my right arm in such a way that my picking—which is my strongest point—would get tired. The ES-330 has a nice thin body, so I don't have that problem.

What kind of amp do you use?

I have a Polytone, which is kind of like a Fender Twin Reverb, except the Twin is much too heavy for me. I can't pick one up, so I use the Polytone. I'd much rather use a tube amp, though.

As one of the few young women in the jazz field, do you have any suggestions or advice for other young women who want to go into jazz?

The first thing is to not get discouraged or bitter about some of the reactions you might get. Just keep playing with conviction, because,at first you're going to have to prove yourself every time you play. Try to be the greatest player you can be. There will be many times when you won't get hired, or when you do get the job, the guys will look at you with faces that show panic, because they think that you're going to play folk music and screw everything up while they're trying to play jazz. You have to stay cool. Be nice to everybody, and you can do more for yourself by playing well. Be confident in yourself. Just realize that the music is everything, and it has nothing to do with politics or the women's liberation movement. *—Excerpted from the September 1981 issue of* Guitar Player

Jimmie Rivers

BY DAN FORTE | MARCH 1996

"THE DANCING STARTS AT NINE AND THE FIGHTS START AT
ten," Jimmie Rivers tells the audience at the 23 Club on the CD reissue of *Brisbane Bop*. And though he was known for his sense of humor, that was no joke.

"If you didn't have a couple of good fights," the guitarist recalls, "the night wasn't a success. I was there for several years, sometimes six nights a week. The boss fired me every other night, and every other night I quit. But I was packing his joint every night."

Rivers' fiery mix of Charlie Christian and Bob Wills was the perfect accompaniment to those brawls. Culled from tapes recorded between 1961 and '64 by steel guitarist Vance Terry in the industrial town south of San Francisco, *Brisbane Bop* was released on vinyl in 1983 on Western Records and eventually became a cult item, prompting its CD release on the Joaquin label. Though the repertoire runs the jazz gamut from the Benny Goodman and Artie Shaw combos to post-bop saxophonist Art Pepper's "Surf Ride," it's labeled "western swing."

"That's what I was supposed to be playing," explains Rivers, "but you can tell we did very little pure country. And we never did play to the audience, per se. The deal was to have fun."

The Oklahoman learned violin from his father, but switched to guitar at age 6 and by 12 was "screwing around with leads."

"We had an old Philco radio that ran off a car battery," the 70-year-old recounts. "We were eight miles from town and had no car, so we were very selective in what we listened to because we had to carry that damn battery all the way to town to get it charged. So my exposure to music was the Bob Wills show on KVOO out of Tulsa every day."

Early guitar influences were Junior Bernard and Eldon Shamblin from the Wills band and the Lightcrust Doughboys' Zeke Campbell. When he moved to Oakland, California, in 1942, Rivers' ears perked up to jazz.

"When I was 16, I tried to sneak in to see a guy named Rudy Sooter. I got thrown out, but one night the band was standing outside because their amplifier went out. I said, 'I've got one you can use!' I ran home four blocks and carried the damn thing back, so they snuck me in the back door. Later the accordionist, Don Burke, said, 'Would you like to play a song?' And they handed the guitar back behind the curtain and we did 'Honeysuckle Rose.' He said, 'You've listened to a lot of Charlie Christian, haven't you?' I said, 'Who's Charlie Christian?' The next day he played me some of Charlie's records, and I went out of my mind. I understood everything he played, because that happened to be the style that just felt natural to me. As a result, I could learn his solos note for note. He was such a genius. God knows what he'd have been if he'd lived longer."

"My exposure to music was the Bob Wills show on KVOO out of Tulsa every day."

Jimmie plays a late '50s Gibson ES-335 but bemoans selling his Epiphone Spartan with a DeArmond pickup—"one of the best sounds I ever got." In 1957 he special-ordered a Gibson doubleneck 6/12 that was stolen from the 23 Club. It turned up on the collectors' market after 29 years and was pictured in the April '95 *Vintage Gallery* magazine.

After his wife passed away in 1964, Rivers didn't touch a guitar until the late '70s. "It felt good," he says, "although you can never come back, technique-wise, to where you were originally after you lay off that long."

He played Dixieland with the Fulton Street Jazz Band, and in the early '80s toured Europe with jazz stalwarts Wild Bill Davison, Peanuts Hucko, and Jay McShann and recorded *Jazz Guitar, Free & Easy*.

Jimmie's a bit awed by the interest in recordings he made 30 years ago. The Brisbane City Council declared a Jimmie Rivers Day last August, but Rivers was unfortunately undergoing surgery. He plays Sundays at Powell's Steamer near his home in Placerville, California, and plans are afoot for an instructional video and maybe another CD. Because of his arthritis, he says, "It would have to be totally different, because I can't cut the fast tempos anymore. But I'd like to make it interesting, with a little more balls to it." —*Excerpted from the March 1996 issue of* Guitar Player

Allison Robertson

BY MICHAEL MOLENDA | JANUARY 2005

THE SAD REASON THAT ESCAPING THE SINS OF YOUR PAST is so not a matter of growing up, maturing, or experiencing a life-changing event is because it's those who remember who we were that trap us in the grasp of history. For example, if your best childhood friends remember you as a preadolescent bed wetter, you can be assured that every action you take and every decision you make as an adult will be assessed in the context of someone emotionally injured by the act of creating lakes in his or her sheets. Or if you cried every time the Coyote got his ass kicked by the Roadrunner, your parents will freeze dry that image of a "sensitive" child weeping at Saturday cartoons in their brains forever—even if you grow up to be Donald Trump.

The Donnas suffer from a similarly unjust twist of fate, but only because they loved music and were ambitious enough to start a punkish girl band in 1993, when the four Palo Alto, California, buddies were still in the eighth grade. It also didn't help that after performing as Ragady Anne and later the Electrocutes, the band assumed a Ramones-ripped identity as the Donnas, complete with identical first names. Cute. And thus the giddy, punk pajama party persona of the band was sealed.

However, guitarist Allison Robertson, vocalist Brett Anderson, bassist Maya Ford, and drummer Torry Castellano haven't used their Donna R., Donna A., Donna F., and Donna C. appellations for some time now, and they pretty much tanked the adorable punk routine with the '70s and '80s guitar-rock influences of 2001's *The Donnas Turn 21.* In addition, Robertson is an obsessive student of classic rock, hard rock, and metal guitar, and her "homework" definitely guided the raw punch of 2002's *Spend the Night* and the rifferific majesty of this year's *Gold Medal.*

Led by a guitarist who lives and breathes heaviness, the Donnas, version 2005, is eons removed from any suggestion of sugary chicks, punk cutesy pies, or pop geeks.

"Everything we do—from the music we play to the guitar and amp I use to our business decisions to what we say in interviews—is done with the thought of how it will affect the future of female acts."

This is a band that rocks hard, and Robertson is a viciously white-hot guitarist. Listen. Learn. Live for today. The Donnas rule.

How do you assess whether you've written a truly kick-ass song?

Whether it's one of our songs or someone else's, what usually makes a song speak to me is the chord progression, how everything fits together, and whether the tune captures a mood.

Were there any creative epiphanies that inspired you to experiment with the Donnas' songcraft for the new album?

What really opened things up was slowing down the tempos—which was partly due to Torry's tendonitis [the condition appeared while the band was rehearsing for Lollapalooza 2003]. She was still recovering from surgery when we began the rehearsal sessions for *Gold Medal* in 2004, and we played the songs slower so as not to tax her too much. As a result, the songs have a real groove instead of always being driving, relentless, and in your face. As a guitarist, that openness allowed me to explore parts that had more funk and feeling.

Also, for this album, I found that I didn't really care if something I wrote wasn't a so-called Donnas' song. I came up with a few things for *Gold Medal* that I thought the band might think were too weird, but I was wrong—they liked the songs because they were different. And while it was a little scary to go for something we hadn't explored before, that very exercise kind of summed up the record. It was like, "Who cares about what we were before, or what people think we are? I'm just gonna write what sounds good in my mind, and I'm gonna do what I feel is creative and different from our last record." Too many bands that we admire just keep churning out something that sounds like their first record.

There are also some sonic alterations on the new record. For example, you are known for pretty much being a guitar-straight-into-the-amp player, but I hear quite a few stompboxes in the mix.

I've never actually been against pedals, but to tell you the truth, we've seldom had the studio time available to experiment with different things, and I've never wanted to just slap something on without taking the time to really work the effect into my style and tone. For this album, I wanted each track to have its own mood, so right from the beginning, I said I wanted to check out a bunch of pedals—especially some delays. I tried not to hit you in the face with the effects, though, because I wanted them to blend with my normal tones. I still can't get over that thing about reproducing my recorded tones onstage, so I didn't want a particular solo to depend on a specific pedal if I decided not to bring that pedal on the road. When you finish making an album, all those sounds are engraved in your brain exactly as they are on the record, and if what I play live doesn't sound like what I remember, I think that I suck. For this very reason, I'll probably bring a Small Stone and a Memory Man on tour.

And it seems an SG has replaced the Les Paul as your guitar of choice.

Yeah. Although I didn't like my SG as much as I'd hoped I would when I first received it. In fact, it was my least favorite guitar, so I had it sitting around my house. I didn't need it at the studio, and I didn't need it on the road, so I left it behind. But it was home when I was writing *Gold Medal*, and I ended up getting addicted to it. It sounds fat and fuzzy and awesome, and it nails that late-'60s, psychedelic tone that I love. No matter what I plug that guitar into, it always delivers a special, very magical tone that's extremely cool.

Are you still using your Marshall?

A lot of the rhythm tones are two guitars played through different amps and panned stereo. I typically put my Marshall JCM 2000 on one side of the mix, and a Fender Vibrolux combo on the other. Sometimes, I'd run the Vibrolux through my Marshall cabinets, and other times, we'd just mic the combo. The Vibrolux glistens with this great distortion that cleans up real nice when you lighten up your attack. It really made the P-90s on my SG sparkle.

How has the guitarist on *Gold Medal* evolved from the guitarist on the last Donnas album, *Spend the Night*?

The guitarist on *Gold Medal* is someone who doesn't care about impressing anyone but herself. This isn't an arrogant statement. It's just that I think I've finally matured as a player. I don't feel like I have to be showy or fast or reinvent anything. I just want each song to set a mood and each solo to tell a story. It's not like this anymore: "Hey, check me out—I'm wanking off." In the past, I always wanted to throw in something just to show people I could do it. That had something to do with being young and immature, and it also had something to do with being a girl. You're never good enough.

It's a drag that sexism has to be one of the factors that drives your will to improve.

Listen, a lot of people still can't get past the fact we can play. With guy bands, that's a given. But we get so much flack that it has absolutely compelled us to try to be heavier, play more complicated riffs, and write things that haven't been written before. Trust me, if you're a woman, you don't want someone saying, "Oh, they're just girls ripping off the same old riffs." Then there are some people who say, "Everyone acts like the Donnas are so good, but they only get all the attention because, compared to other female musicians, they can play their instruments pretty well. But if they were guys, they'd suck."

Ouch!

Oh man, here's another thing that drives us crazy: Any time we do something that's intentionally ironic or kitschy it's considered a gimmick, and we get blasted for it. But, you know, put a guy band in matching outfits and it's considered pure genius. It's even funnier to us when those bands copy, say, the Kinks, and pretend they're doing something awesome that has never been done before. Usually, they're just taking the music to a lamer level, but they often get respected for being "archivists of classic rock."

Do you think female rock acts and women guitarists will ever achieve popular parity with their male counterparts?

Probably not in our lifetime, but one of the goals of our band is to help break down that wall brick-by-brick. Everything we do—from the music we play to the guitar and amp I use to our business decisions to what we say in interviews—is done with the thought of how it will affect the future of female acts. When you're in our position, if you do one thing that makes you look stupid, then it makes all girls look stupid. Whenever some female in the music industry does something too girly or shoots off her mouth and sounds like a dodo, it takes ten years off my life!

As you're a pretty serious student of guitar rock, what's your take on the current state of the genre?

Old-school guitar has been taking a major nose dive for years. Today, everything is edited and Pro Tooled and weighed down with effects. And every time I see someone's rig in a guitar magazine, it's like, "Oh my God, there are ten racks of crazy stuff up there. Doesn't anyone just play through an amp anymore?" I get kind of crazy about that stuff because, with everything in the music industry being so fake, recreated, fixed, or touched up, I look at the guitar as the last thing that can be organic and human. I like it when guitarists leave in mistakes and a little bit of sloppiness, but those are things from the past. Guitar players like Ritchie Blackmore, Jimmy

Page, Tony Iommi, George Harrison, Keith Richards, and Mick Ronson weren't perfect, but they played with a lot of feeling and vibe. Those guys were not hammering out some b.s.

I think it also hurts guitar rock that the grunge backlash hasn't died down—that all the players were sloppy and lame and they covered up their crap with fuzzboxes. To me, however, Kurt Cobain was the epitome of a really cool, interesting guitar player. A lot of people say he was no virtuoso, but you know what? He was probably playing cooler stuff than you were! Kurt went against the grain and showed guitarists that they didn't have to be technical charlatans, and I really wish more of today's players would be just as rebellious. —*Excerpted from the January 2005 issue of* Guitar Player

Sabicas

BY BILL BARTOLINI | DECEMBER 1971

WHEN AUGUSTIN CASTELLON WAS A YOUNG BOY IN SPAIN, he was quite fond of *habas*, a legume similar to lima beans, and would steal them from his mother's kitchen. She would find him and yell, "Habas, habicas!"—habicas being the diminutive form of habas. And since the "h" is silent in Spanish, when "Habas, habicas" is run together, you get the sound "Sabicas."

Sabicas has become synonymous with flamenco guitar. He has recorded almost 50 albums, has toured the United States successfully for 31 years, has received his country's Medal of Honor for having contributed more to Spain's cultural life than anyone else, and is generally regarded as the world's greatest living flamenco guitarist.

Like many artists who have come up the hard way over a period of many years to reach the top of their profession, Sabicas is a man of strong opinions. His feelings of his position as the founder of solo flamenco playing may be disputed by some but will be supported by just as many others. But Sabicas approaches his life as he approaches his music—with his whole being.

The following interview was conducted in Spanish over a period of two days spent during the artist's most recent California tour.

What was your first instrument when you were a child?

A guitar, always a guitar. It was a little guitar that I got when I was about five years old. I picked it up and started playing it—making noise—and my family would remind me to be kind to my mother, because at 5 a.m., I'd be strumming away, and no one could get any sleep. Later, I got a bigger instrument, and when I was eight, I made my debut in town, in Pamplona, during the pledge to the flag. I came out to play, and it was a scandal when people saw me. The curtain went up, and out came a little mousy kid, with my school apron and my guitar. People were rolling in the aisles. They wouldn't let me play, they were laughing so hard. When I *did* start, they threw me pesetas and other coins. They never hit the ground. I'd get up and catch them in the air and continue playing. I filled my pockets with pesetas—about 100 in all. Everybody was happy with that concert. That's how I started.

Then, by 1937, you had your own company, and you left Spain to tour.

Yes. We went to Buenos Aires. Beautiful city. Beautiful country. We liked it very much there, and stayed until 1940. In Buenos Aires was the great dancer Carmen Amaya—glory be to her. She was a revolution all by herself! Tickets were sold for three months in advance. And after three months of playing, there were tickets sold for the next three months. It was a wonder—a scandal. People were enchanted by it. And how the guitar is liked in that country!

Do you think of yourself as a gypsy?

Yes, sir.

People who write about the history of flamenco have said that its roots are in the folk music of Spain, plus contributions from the Moors, Jews, and so on, and that upon this base, the gypsies build more of the edifice of flamenco. But they say that the gypsies have not added any new forms.

The forms that exist in flamenco have been created by gypsies. We came out of India around 1500. We went to Europe, and many of us stayed in Spain. We liked Andalucia most of all. We started to work as blacksmiths. The hammer and the anvil is where the singing began. Flamenco singing, against what many books say, is of Spain. The gypsies started to sing without the guitar, because there was no flamenco guitar. I don't think the flamenco guitar is older than about 130 years. At first, very little was done on the guitar. The singers all had to stay in the same key, since the capo was not then known. So they had to sing in *E* or *D* or *B*, until one day, a guitar player thought of using a pencil tied with string on the first or second fret. Then the singer he was accompanying found he could raise his voice more—could sing in his natural range. At first, the singing was in the houses of Andalucia, without charging money—just for pleasure. Then it was taken to the Cafe Cantantes—the songs, the dances, the guitar. Then it was taken to the stage and the theatre, and so on until today.

Do you play any contemporary music?

Everything I play is mine. Flamenco has no written music. That's why it's extremely difficult. For other types of guitar playing, almost everything is down on paper. It tells one how to play it, where to put the fingers, slowly here, loudly there. In flamenco, there is no one to tell you anything. Everything is by intuition, by one's own taste, out of one's heart, by invention. And it's very difficult. As time goes by, I see the guitar growing more difficult because it isn't enough to just play the guitar. It's three careers in one: One career is to play for the singer, another is to play for the dancer, and another is to play—"by earned right," as we say.

Now, one who knows a lot—who does a lot of different things on the guitar—this man probably does not play flamenco. That is, he plays many things that are well liked but worthless because he does not play flamenco. It seems as if they do very little on the guitar, yet they do more than those who play so much.

You're talking about simple but deep playing, then?

Exactly. They are people who know. Masters they are called. A singer comes, they play perfectly. A dancer comes, same thing. What they play is what *must* be played. Instead of doing a lot of things badly, it's better to do little but well. Flamenco is a thing that requires time. Young

> *"Flamenco has no written music. That's why it's extremely difficult."*

people, they want to race the guitar. They have their youth—they have the fever of the guitar. But when one realizes what the guitar is and what one must wring from it is its sweetness—well, that's the most difficult thing to achieve, On the guitar you must have, above all, a good sound, and as the years go by, you realize that racing leads nowhere. The challenge is to play sweetly and pleasingly at the right tempo.

Since you have made two albums with rock musicians, do you feel rock is approaching the sophistication of flamenco, and do you find a confluence between the two?

Yes. In those two fields I believe great things can be done. It is rhythmic, and I believe great things can be realized here.

How long do you wear your nails?

As short as possible. The shorter the nail, the surer the playing. It's louder and has a better sound. With a lot of nail, it sounds like a *bandurria* [a steel-strung, mandolin-like instrument]. The sound is much too bright. The nail needs some flesh so that the sound can be sweet—so that it can come out pleasant.

Do you enamel them?

I use a little bit so that they last longer. Faberge. It's a little thick, but it lasts.

When you do a normal *rasgueo*, you use four fingers downward?

Yes, sometimes. In others, three and even two.

When you tap, does your tapping depend on where you are playing? Does it cover a wide arc of the soundboard or do you restrict it?

Normally, in the same place close to the bridge, about three centimeters from it.

How do you see the future of flamenco?

Better—ever better. It has spread so well. For example, the first recording I did 16 years ago in New York, the publishers tell me the top sales in the whole world were in Japan. I could hardly believe it. I would have thought Spain or some Latin country.

From your vantage point on the top of the mountain, so to speak, what sort of development do you see in the flamenco artists of today?

The normal development of today's flamenco artists is based on things of my own. Today, the guitarist has a lot of fingers. They play a lot—the young ones. They study a lot. They play with a terrible fury and very well. Now then, I've come out with a new technique and everyone is playing this. They change it a little bit, it's natural not to make it exactly the same, but anyway, it's Sabicas they are playing. Thirty years ago there were far fewer guitarists, but those that were around played in a different way, within flamenco. Flamenco is a very personal thing. And, as in any art, one must not imitate anyone. Now, if you imitate someone else, even if you do it better, the name and the fanfare is still for the author. When you do things of your own, they are worthwhile. —*Excerpted from the December 1971 issue of* Guitar Player

Sonny Sharrock

BY MARK DERY | FEBRUARY 1990

"BEAUTY WILL BE CONVULSIVE OR WILL NOT BE AT ALL"
is the last emphatic, fist-shaking line in Andre Breton's surrealist romance *Nadja*, but it could have been written by Sonny Sharrock. In fact, the guitarist expressed a similar sentiment in his February 1989 *Guitar Player* article on free improvisation when he adjured players to pursue beauty, "be it the fragile beauty of a snowflake, or the terrible beauty of an erupting volcano."

Some critics, like the one who compared Sharrock's fretwork to "shards of splintered glass," have chosen to underscore that "terrible" quality, forgetting that the asterisk of cracks in a shattered windshield can be as beautiful as a snowflake in its own jagged way. After all, isn't the stained-glass window in a Gothic cathedral, dazzling when the sun makes its colors catch fire, just so much splintered glass? Sharrock's guitar-playing is like stained glass—ragged-edged and razor-sharp, but possessed of a burning beauty.

To be sure, the beauty that Sharrock has pursued through the years on records by Herbie Mann, Pharoah Sanders, Miles Davis, and Bill Laswell—as well as his own—has been unorthodox. And he has sought that unorthodox beauty with unorthodox techniques. Sharrock is a musical polyglot, and his style bears the stamp of a dozen-odd influences. Using a lap-steel bar slide, he tosses off machine-gunned double-stops that harken to Blind Willie Johnson and mewling glissandi that mimic the squeaks and squeals of Pharoah Sanders' saxophone. His heavily accented, highly syncopated strumming recalls Bo Diddley, while his shuffling, behind-the-beat rhythms echo New Orleans stride pianist Professor Longhair. In his single-note lines, he combines volume, distortion, and percussive picking to create pitches so rich in overtones that they sound almost chordal, recalling the multiphonic melodies of saxman Ornette Coleman.

"I'm a romantic," says Sharrock, "and there are certain feelings that hurt good. That's what I'm trying to reach. I want to create a feeling with what I play—something that hurts."

Nearing 50, Sharrock is amused to find himself the grand old man of "out" guitar, the damn-the-torpedoes unorthodoxy and sweat-drizzling fury of his playing an inspiration to a new generation of noisemakers. Ironically, he is, by his own admission, becoming more melodic as the years go by. He must sometimes wonder what younger players would think if they knew that the man whose solos sound like a handful of nuts, bolts, and ball bearings zinging around in a washing machine still dreams of being a doo-wop star.

You've said that you first started playing freely while accompanying Miles Davis' "Milestones." Technically speaking, how did your style change?

Well, I started picking very heavily. These days, I pick so heavily that I break strings. I pick slower, too, but picking heavily has so much more feeling. When I hit a string, especially on record, you can hear three or four notes. There's the note comes from where my left hand is placed, as well as from the pick action. It gives a hell of a sound to each note. And then I run it all through distortion.

I was in a local music store the other day, and a guy came in with a guitar he wanted to have fixed to give him a particular sound. I had to leave the room, because I almost laughed in this guy's face. I think of myself as a horn player, and horn players rely on their *embouchure* [the position of the lips] to give them their particular sound. That's what makes Sonny Rollins different from Coltrane and Charlie Parker different from Benny Carter. So, as a guitarist who always thought he was a horn player, I always believed the sound was in my hands—not in the electronic boxes or the internal circuitry of the guitar. I can play a Les Paul, an ES-175, or whatever and get the same sound, because it's all in my hands. Each player has the sound in his hands, and if he doesn't have the sound in his hands, he ain't playin' sh*t!

Generally, though, it's all in the right hand. I alternate-pick with a heavy slapping action. I'm very noisy—very dirty. I've tried to decrease some of the dirt by holding the pick with the fingers out—like an "okay" sign. I have to use a big pick, because I pick so hard that if I use smaller ones, I lose or break them. I go through a lot of picks in a night. I use a triangular pick, rotating it around the triangle. The best are those black Gibson mediums—they just get a nicer tone.

You've made it clear that harmony doesn't interest you much. At the same time, you consider yourself a jazz player. How do you reconcile those attitudes, considering that so much jazz guitar is chordally oriented?

Well, look at the size of my fingers—they're like little sausages! I can't do those extended chords. Also, you need that really clean tone to play those chords, and I obviously don't have that. The truth is, I just don't have time for chord substitution.

I think that harmony gets in my way. It clutters things up, and I end up doing formulas instead of trying to reach something. Of course, I love Coltrane—who was the master of harmony—but look at his music towards the end. He had put harmony out at the back door. He was concentrating on playing through one tonal center—or a couple of tonal centers—to reach the thing he was after. He was still a harmonic player, but he had pushed aside the harmonies that he'd been given.

Still, you don't always play single-line melodies. You frequently use Jimmy Reed-style double-stops, or droning open strings juxtaposed with fretted notes in a way that recalls country blues.

Well, the guitar naturally lends itself to those things. When I first started doing that back in the '60s, double-stops and droning strings were a blues thing. Nobody had done it in a jazz way. But I always admired the sound of those effects and thought they were just a natural part of the instrument.

That drone thing is definitely inherent to the guitar. I used to work a lot with playing fretted notes against open strings, although I don't do that as much anymore. I worked out a whole bunch of techniques for doing that, using different tunings that facilitated it. The original recording of "Blind Willie" on *Black Woman* involved tuning all the strings to *E*, in different octaves. Guys used to try to see what I was doing, because they couldn't understand how I got that sound.

I heard this drone sound in my mind, but I didn't want a harmonic drone because I wouldn't be free to go other places. You see, if I had tuned it to one chord, I would have been hampered by that chord. But to tune to one note, and make that the tonal center, left me free to go all over the place.

Players seem to be taking an increasingly pianistic approach to the guitar, using techniques such as two-handed tapping to replicate the wide intervallic spans one can get on a keyboard. Do these developments whet your appetite for chordal playing?

I ain't got *time* for that! I'm trying to reach something in the soul. Jazz—or whatever critics want to call the music I play—is an improvisational music. This tapping thing, where you're dealing with harmony, has to be thought out upfront. It's not directed toward an improvisatory end. Back when I first started listening to jazz, guitar players would do these chord solos, and you knew they weren't improvised. There was no way you could improvise those things. The fingerings just had to be worked out in advance. That is not improvisation, and improvisation is what my music is about. I want to create melody, to create a feeling, something that *hurts*.

How do you feel about the state of jazz guitar today?

Is there such a thing [*laughs*]? Seriously, though, there are some really excellent players out there, and I enjoy what they do. But jazz guitarists aren't so interested in making it hurt—they're more interested in making it clean. The cry of jazz has been forgotten by a lot of people, and that is probably the most important element in jazz. When you are finally able to play after 20 years of practicing, then you get the cry. And when you get that, then you're playing something. But because they play an electric instrument, many guitarists forget that cry. They become interested in making something clean and they lose something.

How do you improvise?

I play the melody, and by the time I reach its end, I want it to have led me to someplace else.

> "*I want to create a feeling with what I play—something that hurts.*"

There's a point where you're walking along the road, and then the road disappears from under your feet. But that doesn't matter, because as you step, the road builds itself. Sometimes, I improvise and play a phrase that's so beautiful—and beauty is the thing I'm after—that it's everything for me. I'll just quit, right then. Other times, I get very bored with what I'm doing, so I just stop. It doesn't take very long for me to get bored with myself. When it's right, on the other hand, I'm just going where the music is leading me. Then it's just a matter of thinking about the feeling I'm working in and making that feeling come out musically. I'm trying to get closer and closer to that pure melody, and whatever it takes to get there, I'll do it. But I don't want to go through a lot of bullsh*t on the way—effects pedals, worrying about the electricity, and all that sh*t.

Like I've said, I just don't have time to think about these things when I'm trying to play, and I don't know who does. I've seen players who stand there, and you can see that their minds are working like an IBM PC, rattling off this sh*t, and I'm always disturbed by that. I hate thinking players! You should know what you're about and just let yourself go. Thinking! I'd rather have an audience that's jumping down on the floor, getting with the music, feeling the music, rather than sitting there with a pipe and all. What is that sh*t? I like it down and dirty! Let's tumble!

Are there ever moments in the middle of an improvisation where you think, "That's it—that's the payoff"? Or is that goal just a mirage that musicians spend their lives chasing?

Well, I know that when I play, I never get it right. And every time, it gets worse for me. There are more things I forgot to say. I'm not talking about notes—I'm talking about feelings. I listen to records or tapes and I hear where I lose it, and I'll say, "Oh, sh*t! I'm just meandering all over the place. What happened?" Trying to make it go the way I want it to go, to make that sound I want to hear, is so difficult, man! Trying to describe it in words—in terms of notes or extensions of harmony or whatever—is just impossible. Maybe if I did realize what I'm after, it would be like Jimmy Swaggart and the rapture, you know. That cat really thinks he's gonna be lifted up when everything goes down.

I'm really just going where the music takes me. I'm not trying to direct it in any way. I don't know if anyone will understand this or not, but the concepts it's leading me to are very still. Of course, the eruptions still happen. There are times when things just explode, and it's all fire—kind of like *The Towering Inferno* with the windows popping out of the building and all that. And then everything just comes back down, and it's still again. But those eruptions have to be there and always will be. You can stop breathing if you get too still. —*Excerpted from the February 1990 issue of* Guitar Player

Earl Slick

BY MICHAEL MOLENDA | NOVEMBER 2004

HE COULD RIP YOUR HEAD OFF IN SO MANY WAYS THAT
the only survivable course of action was complete surrender. He didn't even have
to play more than one note either, because he knew how to hit the right note and
smack it, bend it, and throttle it until every drip of angst and pain was dragged out
of the string and set loose inside your psyche. And when he did play it pretty, it was
beautiful and surprising—ethereal melodies etched with a soaring, sensual tone that
transcended sound and technique and blues and rock to become something visceral,
like a first kiss or a painting that you can't stop staring at.

Yeah, the old Earl Slick was one scary dude, and few guitarists who actually give a
toss about passion and intensity could experience his stage work with David Bowie—
specifically *David Live* and the video of the *Serious Moonlight* tour—without folding in
on themselves like a wet shoebox. Add his spine-tingling rock riffs on Bowie's *Station
to Station* (brilliantly juxtaposed with coguitarist Carlos Alomar's funk stabs), his tune-
ful swagger on John Lennon's *Double Fantasy*, and the guitar party of *Phantom, Rocker
& Slick*, and you've got one awesome repertoire of 6-string genius.

But that was then. After taking a break from the music industry in the early '90s,
Slick emerged healthy and as ambitious as ever (he even started his own record
label, Slick Music), but he was uninterested in reigniting the stunning displays of
virtuosity that distinguished his past work. "I got bored, man," he admits. "I just got
bored sick with all of that guitar-hero stuff."

Indeed, the new Earl Slick—who reunited with Bowie in 2000—is more about tone and texture than woo-woo-diddley-wahhh. His most recent solo album, last year's *Zig Zag*, is a fabulous mixture of vibey rock instrumentals and songs with guest vocalists (including Robert Smith, Joe Elliot, Roy Langdon, Martha Davis, and Bowie) that's exciting and impassioned—even when its main man refuses to go off. In fact, the album was originally conceived partly as a calling card for film soundtrack work, which accounts for its edgy melodicism and cinematic tonal layers.

Of course, some fans may yearn for the Slick of old, and he acknowledges this without rancor or regret. But the Slick talking and smoking as he shows me a new Burns guitar in his room at San Francisco's Four Seasons hotel this summer is extremely happy, creatively charged up, and still crazy about gear. We should all be so lucky.

I have to say that if I had your talents, it would be hard for me to relinquish such an identifiable approach to soloing. But you let it all go so freely.

One of the reasons I took that break in the '90s was that I found myself in this box of "blues-rock guitar player." Now, without a doubt, that's an aspect of what I do, but there are other aspects to my style that I wasn't getting called to do. It seemed like I was being directed by this reputation, and it became more and more difficult to clear my head and think about music from a different point of view. It's nothing against anybody I worked with, but that's the way it was. So I became very frustrated, because I wasn't enjoying the blues-rock stuff anymore, and I wanted to experiment. I wanted to explore a moodier direction.

I think the last thing I did the "old" way was *In Your Face*, the solo album I released in 1991. That record was basically conceived as a collection of tracks for me to solo over. But by the time I was ready to do *Zig Zag*, I was sick and tired of that stuff.

Still, *Zig Zag* is one hell of a guitar record—even given that it's solo light.

I think the reason is that this album, probably more than any album I've ever done, came almost purely from an emotional point of view. Everything from the chord changes to the guitars I selected to play on each song was driven by however I was feeling when I sat down to write and record.

Can you be more specific about the emotional context of the record?

Well, the way my brain operates is that music is like a mood-altering drug to me. It puts me in an emotional space. So if I'm listening to Link Wray, for example, what he does will put me in a certain mood, and that mood will inspire me to write. From there, all I usually have to do is get some kind of twangy tone going on with the guitar, and then my frame of mind takes over and does all the rest. It's kind of a weird way to write, because it's not calculated.

As you've been touring with Bowie again, aren't you tempted to pull out some of the old *David Live* histrionics?

[*Laughs.*] No! This is the way I enjoy playing now. I love messing around with sounds and doing things in a more simple manner. Also, I've gotten very inspired by playing within song structures rather than soloing over them. This is probably due to the fact that I understand song forms better because I've been writing more myself. And—believe me—I am sick and tired of the chops thing!

Okay, I believe you. But can you at least detail how you approached your performances with the '70s Bowie, as opposed to the 2004 Bowie?

Back in the day, it was about not staying too close to the structure and doing lots of soloing. Nowadays, I'm more apt to cop some stock parts. I'll still add my edge to those parts—and I do all the rhythm stuff my own way—but I'm playing a lot less of the dramatic solos. I'm doing stuff like catching two strings and hitting them for the entire solo. Anything I'm doing is still aggressive, but there are a lot less notes. I'm playing a lot more with my sounds than I am with my chops.

"A perfect guitar solo never got me a platinum album."

If you wanted guitarists to experience the best of Earl Slick, what albums would you direct them to?

Off the top of my head, they would be *Double Fantasy* [John Lennon], *Station to Station* and *Reality* [David Bowie], and *Zig Zag*.

What gear are you currently using?

I have an Ampeg Dan Armstrong, an ESP loaded with DiMarzio Fast Tracks and a Fernandes Sustainer, a Fender Stratocaster, a double-cutaway Gibson Les Paul Classic, some Gibson Les Paul Standards with Bigsbys, a Gibson Firebird, a custom Peavey with three single-coils, a '69 Gibson J-45, and a Tacoma 12-string acoustic. My current amp setup is two Ampeg Reverberocket 50-watt heads with Ampeg 4x12 cabinets. It's a great amp and there's nothing to it! My effects include a Boss DD-3 Digital Delay, an old and a new Ibanez Tube Screamer, an Ibanez CF7 Stereo Chorus/Flanger, an Ibanez DE7 Stereo Delay/Echo, a Line 6 DL4 Delay Modeler, and a Voodoo Lab Micro Vibe. My strings are Dean Markley, gauged .010–.048.

You've revealed that the original, all-instrumental version of *Zig Zag* was conceived as a demo for film work—how would you approach soundtrack composition?

If the director didn't have a preconceived idea about the music, I'd probably just watch the film with a guitar in my hands. I'd play whatever comes into my head—while simultaneously recording the rough ideas to a cassette machine—and then develop the ideas later. That's the thing with me: Whatever happens first is what it is.

You mean you don't ever run through a bunch of takes until a part is absolutely perfect?

No way. There's working hard and there's working smart, and some people think if something's not painful, it's not good—like doing the same solo for three days in a row until it's perfect. I can think of better things to do.

Why do you think it's so difficult for many guitarists to trust their instincts?

I think it's a combination of things, but it usually comes down to ego. If a player is unsure of himself or afraid of criticism, then he'll always worry someone will say a part is a little out of tune, or that they bent a note too much or too little. I don't care. I figure it's like this: I'm going to do what I'm going to do, and some people are going to like it, and some people aren't going to like it. A perfect guitar solo never got me a platinum album.

It's that old question of feel over technique again, isn't it?

Yeah, but it's more than that. I look at playing guitar as a complete artistic work, where the player has to have the tone, the look, the clothes, and the right guitar. That's the big reason I gravitate to guitarists such as Link Wray or Jet's Nic Cester—they have the whole package going on. I mean, Nic plays simple, gritty, primal, in-your-face guitar, and he totally looks the part. Now, I'm not saying there isn't room for someone who is solely an amazing player, but I come from a place where rock and roll is about expression, not just technique.

Donita Sparks

BY MICHAEL MOLENDA | DECEMBER 1999

"OUR BASIC TRIP IS DISTORTION," SAYS L7 GUITARIST

Donita Sparks, "but we always feel free to throw in something fresh, strange, or goofy." On *Slap-Happy*, the inaugural release from L7's own label, Sparks and coguitarist Suzi Gardner mingle bloops, bleeps, quacks, and other noises with a fuzz palette that ranges from big and ballsy to thin and spitty. Depending on the song, the duo's distorted tones can sweep from '70s glam to '90s grunge to a "Black Sabbath meets Hole" hybrid. But whatever the fuzz flavor might be, it's not the result of a pedal plugged into a cranked amp.

"There may not be an amazing player in the lineup, but the band is a contender."

"A distortion pedal through a Marshall sounds like crap," says Sparks. "The tone is always real scratchy—not beefy at all. It's like the distortion of the Marshall cancels out the pedal. It's best to run fuzz pedals through a Fender and keep the amp's tone clean."

Sparks plugs an Epiphone Flying V or MDX Custom Flying V ("I've always played Flying Vs—they look hilarious and sound right for our music") into a '65 50-watt Fender Bassman head and Hiwatt 4x12 cabinet. Although she uses a Maestro Fuzz and other vintage stompboxes in the studio, Sparks opts for Boss HM-3 Hyper Metal, FZ-3 Fuzz, and GE-7 Graphic EQ pedals on the road.

"We're not the best players in the world," she admits, "but we go for the soul—it's all about the songs and spirit, rather than technical expertise. I mean, a lot of talented guitarists just don't rock me. And while I respect players who can play, there's something to be said for bands like us who rock as a unit. There may not be an amazing player in the lineup, but the band is a contender."

John Sykes

BY MATT BLACKETT | NOVEMBER 2001

ALTHOUGH AT THE TIME, WHITESNAKE HAD BEEN AROUND
for almost ten years, their eponymous 1987 release made the band an overnight sensation, and it put the guitar playing of John Sykes squarely in the public's face. But while Sykes cowrote nearly every song on *Whitesnake*—including the crushing "Still of the Night"—he split acrimoniously with the band before the album's release.

"I regret that I never got to play those songs live—and I think the fans regret it, too," says Sykes, who released *Nuclear Cowboy* last year (available at johnsykes.com) and is currently reforming his band, Blue Murder.

> *"I regret that I never got to play those songs live—and I think the fans regret it, too."*

"For the rhythm on 'Still of the Night,' I used my 1978 black Les Paul Custom," he says. "At that time, I had a Gibson Dirty Fingers pickup in the bridge. I plugged into two Mesa/Boogie Coliseums—which are great-sounding amps. I ran the gain at about four, so the tone was heavy but clear. I cut my rhythm tracks as Aynsley Dunbar laid down the drums, and I tracked in stereo with a slight delay between the two sides. Then I doubled the part."

After the brutal power chords and single-note riffing in the verse and chorus, "Still of the Night" features a moody breakdown section.

"The clean stuff was my 1961 Strat," says Sykes. "I didn't use an amp—I just plugged into some outboard gear for the compression, chorus, and reverb and ran direct. Although the signature line sounds like it had some slapback, it doesn't—I just palm muted the notes as I played them. I used a Charvel for the trem-bar part."

The end of the breakdown contains a stunning solo that showcases Sykes' mind-boggling shred chops.

"I used my Les Paul and a 50-watt Marshall that was modified by Jose Arredondo," he explains. "The Marshall tone was a little sweeter, and it had a little more sustain than the Boogies. I used some right-hand muting to keep the notes clean and just went for it. I don't like to have every note worked out beforehand. I wasn't around for the mix, and [Whitesnake vocalist] David Coverdale mixed the solo way too low. I think that's a shame, because there's some nice stuff in there—especially the ascending runs—but you really have to strain to hear everything. He also added delay and reverb, which buries the solo even further into the mix. I don't hold any grudges, though. The vibe in the studio for that record was great, the band represented a special time in my life, and this song is a good piece of work. I'm proud of it."

The Great Kat

BY MICHAEL MOLENDA | SEPTEMBER 2002

INTERVIEWING THE GREAT KAT IS MUCH LIKE HURTLING
through some Grand Guignol anime death match where you just barely survive a
punch-up with flesh-shredding hell spawn, only to have a dump truck fall on your
head as you're resting and licking your wounds. If the preceding seems a little over
the top, please consider that *Webster's* offers no appropriate word or phrase to describe this woman's intensity. She talks faster than she plays, and she can zoom up
and down a fretboard faster than a hungry cheetah on steroids. She also yells a lot.
And she demands attention—which means an interviewer can pretty much forget
about interjecting, interrupting, or sucking in a breath or two.

The Great Kat's ferocious passion is unleashed in the service of a divine mission:
zapping her ultra-virtuosic, 22nd-century shred classical concept into the synapses
of what she calls the "moron masses." To accomplish this, the Juilliard-trained violinist and guitar shredder transforms classical masterworks into speed-metal songs,
rages like a demented dominatrix, spews blood, bears arms, exposes her goodies,
and indulges in both mental and dramatic castrations.

Now, if you're thinking about giggling—*don't*. Some may feel The Great Kat looks
and acts like a freak, but if so, she's a freak who can outplay just about every guitarist on the planet. (Go ahead and challenge her—she'll prove it!) In addition,
her work ethic would bring most players to their knees. She builds her meticulous
shred-classical adaptations of Wagner, Vivaldi, and Beethoven by entering the origi-

nal scores *note-by-note* into Sibelius music-notation software before rearranging the works for guitar.

"The guitar will not always match the sound quality of the violins, violas, and cellos, so you have to change the register, the fingering positions, and certain notes so that the score fits within the playing capabilities of the guitar," she explains. "I work out the arrangements on violin first—which often requires six months of practice, going 12 hours a day to master one minute of music. Then I play the work on the guitar. I edit out the boring stuff, keep the main themes, and speed everything up. It's an overwhelming task, but it's the only way to get people who are used to listening to Bugs Bunny music to be excited and engaged by the works of geniuses."

The Great Kat's total commitment to her art and craft hasn't left her much bandwidth for a supportive and nurturing presence. She's not shy about dissing "lazy" women, badgering dilettantes of both sexes, or trumpeting her fearsome speed-power majesty. In The Great Kat's world, lesser guitarists can get better, get out of her way, or bow in worship. Make your choice.

"I'm trying to make musicians realize that to become brilliant players, you need brilliant music."

Hello?

THIS IS THE WHOLE INTERVIEW RIGHT HERE! Guys have dicks, and therefore guys can be considered guitar heroes. Females have no dicks, and that means guys cannot worship them. Guys cannot say that The Great Kat FEMALE is a guitar hero. Because if they ever said, "Wow, that's amazing—I love what she does on guitar," their little dicks would shrivel off. ARE YOU GETTING THIS? This is the WHOLE POINT. All those other guitar magazines don't want to write about The Great Kat, because if I come in and establish the protocol for powerful female guitarists, then all the other bitches behind me are going to come in—*if* they're qualified and are technical virtuosos—and that pathetic one-inch penis WILL NOT define a guitar hero. It will mean NOTHING!

Well, this is a nice start...

Let me tell you something else: Women guitarists don't want to get off their LAZY BITCH ASSES and practice their balls off! Women are not INTERESTED in competing with guys. They start these little bands with other women because THEY CAN'T HACK IT! They're in their tiny little nonthreatening groups that will NEVER EVER SCARE THE CRAP OUT OF MEN. You know why? Because they're SCARED of what guys will think if they get TOO DAMN GOOD. Well, I'll *tell* you what the guys will think. They'll say, "You're a ugly dog. We don't want to have sex with you anymore. We hate your guts."

But if a woman doesn't have the capability to compete against men, THEN SHE CAN GO TO HELL! Why do you think some people love me and some people hate me? The ones who love me say, "I accept the fact that I am influenced by The Great Kat, and I will kick ass." But the haters can't do what I can do, and they will never accept the fact they have to get WAY BETTER!

What inspired your concept of shred classical?

After studying at Juilliard, I realized classical music was dead. No one was listening to it. So I looked at what the moron masses were listening to, and I asked myself, "What's the most exciting music?" Metal! Right then and there I decided to mix heavy metal with classical music. But you can't just bring in metal styles and lay them on top of classical music, you must also maintain the virtuosity of true classical genius. This is what defines shred classical. I am systematically, single-handedly taking Juilliard morons to task, and all the classical composers after Beethoven who choked the life out of classical music because they were *not* virtuosos. And I'm not only resurrecting classical music, I'm resurrecting metal—which has been systematically destroyed by all those Metallica-style bands. You have to be able to PLAY, asshole!

At the risk of getting bludgeoned, I have to ask why you feel you need all the sex and gore to promote yourself, when you are quite obviously a brilliant guitarist?

If it takes The Great Kat wearing dominatrix outfits—and DRIPPING IN BLOOD with a whip in my hand—to get people to wake up to shred classical, that's what The Great Kat will do, because The Great Kat is not only updating classical music for the 21st-century morons, I'm also being an entertainer. I'm mixing shred metal and classical music with operatic theater. What I'm doing is, little by little, jamming the genius of Vivaldi and Wagner down their throats while I'm entertaining them with the blood and domination and castration. I AM THE DOMINATRIX OF WAR!

Listen, people are stupid, and they want the easiest formula for their slow-thinking brains. If you give them one ounce of Beethoven, they will THROW UP. People would rather listen to Madonna's crap than Mozart. Now if they were *intelligent*, they would say, "I need to hear the music of geniuses to make me more intelligent—not crap music that makes me stupid." I'm trying to make musicians realize that to become brilliant players, you need brilliant music. We don't have time for years and years to pass by while everybody is sitting around saying, "But I *like* old blues." WAKE UP! It's crap. It's STUPID.

You're pretty down on musical conventions, aren't you?

WELL, AREN'T *YOU* BORED? Listen, if you want to help resurrect guitar—well, first you have to read music. Then you have to study violin books such as Sevcik's *The School of Bowing* and Carl Flesch's *Basic Studies for Violin*, because all the guitar books are doing is teaching you how to play traditional guitar. Now, guitarists don't like me saying stuff like this. But I'm a violin virtuoso who plays guitar, and I also happen to be updating your instrument for you, so THANK YOU VERY MUCH, ASSHOLES! You also need to learn composition, and you have to be able to transcribe.

But you know what? Most guitarists won't do this because people want instantaneous gratification. If it takes them like two minutes to get a chord under their fingers, they're not interested. We've created a world of amateurs and morons who have only learned enough about the guitar to finger some moronically simple riff and write an idiotic song. AREN'T YOU FED UP WITH ALL THIS INFERIORITY? Somebody has to STEP UP! If you want to do something brilliant, you've got to work for it. Doing something that will change the world requires AWESOME TECHNICAL ABILITY. To produce powerful and exciting music YOU MUST BE A VIRTUOSO.

Speaking of virtuousity, how did you develop your stunning speed?

Everyone knows that you practice stuff real slow and then start speeding it up. But *how* I play is different from most guitarists who plop their fingers down flat across the guitar and move around in one position. The Great Kat uses the Paganini technique, which requires that you take your fingers and you make them perfectly perpendicular to the fretboard—like claws. It's totally strict, and the vibrato is extremely tight and fast. It's not like the wide, bend-y vibrato that rock and blues guitarists use. At the speeds I play, I don't have time for that!

Also, my fingering is very light—which is critical to violin performance, because if you play, say, Tchaikovsky's *Violin Concerto*, and your fingering is aggressive and heavy, you'll sound out of tune. You'll also get behind the beat. It's all about being fast and light.

While you are basically destroying old-school classical music by speeding it up and fusing it with metal, you also have a very sweet, sincere, and very deep respect for classical composers.

The reason I respect, admire, and draw strength from Paganini, Beethoven, and the classical masters is because they put up with CRUSHING GODDAMN CRITICISM and they still produced genius. Beethoven, for example, invented "romantic" classical music from a traditional classical music mold left by Mozart. He wasn't afraid of people saying, "Boy, that's noisy!" They said, "We want the calm, relaxing classical music that doesn't insult our senses," and Beethoven comes up with "BAH BAH BAH BAHHHHHH! F**K YOU!" Any musician who establishes a new protocol for music is going to get *tortured*, man. The fearless don't care. They kick ass and move things forward while the COWARDS sit back and play it safe and collect compliments.

Steve Tibbetts

BY JAMES ROTONDI | DECEMBER 2002

WHEN STEVE TIBBETTS RECORDS AN ALBUM, HE DOESN'T
track a dozen clever tunes. Instead, he molds sonic sculptures from gargantuan
sheets of sound. His audio clay consists of shimmering 12-string bends, groan-
ing Strat riffs, and bursts of white-hot feedback layered over rumbling percussion,
spooky drones, and subliminal Zen chanting. Using a recursive process that's as
unique as his music, Tibbetts created *A Man About a Horse* by assembling, manipulating, deconstructing, and then reassembling hundreds of guitar, percussion, and
vocal textures.

"Before touching my Strat or Martin D-12," he says, "I began building rhythms
using the kendang, which is a barrel-shaped Balinese hand drum. Using two ancient
Roland S760s, I sampled taps and slaps from my four drums, and then sequenced
different patterns I'd learned when studying *kebyar*— the gamelan orchestra—in In-
donesia. One pattern, the *gilak*, turned out to be a real gold mine. I'd play it against
itself, offsetting the rhythm by an eighth-note, a sixteenth-note, or a thirty-second
note. I got all the beats on this album from that initial gilak pattern.

"I recorded these sequencer-generated rhythms on my old Tascam MS-16
16-track tape deck—which I love because it lets me work with pitch. For example,
if I want a drum sound that's a minor third or fifth below the original, I raise the
recorder's speed before rolling tape. Then, when I play back at normal speed, the
drum sounds lower. I've made a chart, so I know where to set the speed control

for a specific interval. Like, if I want to drop a drum down a whole-step, I increase the recording speed by 12.2 percent. I go back and forth between the sampler and tape machine so much—looping, cutting, offsetting, and layering—that eventually I don't know where the sounds come from. It's like trying to find your camping spot by looking at a map of North America."

Once he had crafted dozens of grooves, Tibbetts felt ready to wrangle guitar tones. "At that point, it was just a big sandbox," he reveals. "Over different rhythms, I played phrases into the tape machine, the samplers, and MOTU's Digital Performer running on a Power Macintosh, and then worked for days transforming the sounds. I might sample a guitar theme with the S760, shift it down a fourth or fifth with the Tascam, and then slice it up with Digital Performer—maybe creating a fugue-like subject that I'd play against itself in reverse, an octave lower. Then, with my Marshall JCM 800 blasting, I made feedback loops—large swaths of shredding sound—and fattened them with similar tones, including horns I recorded while visiting a Tibetan monastery. They sound like overdriven guitars, but an octave down."

"Instead of new toys, seek new adventures."

Tibbetts uses custom headphones to protect his hearing while tracking feedback assaults.

"The guys at the local gun shop think I'm an avid sharpshooter," he laughs, "because I have five pairs of Browning ear protectors for varying degrees of attenuation. I've stuffed them with drivers from Radio Shack headphones, so I can monitor the recorded tracks. If you want your amp to sound like the speaker coils are starting to spin and fly off, you have to take it to that point. Amp modelers won't do it—they just sound like sophisticated fuzzboxes."

Tibbetts' custom tunings contribute to the churning madness. "I have my Strat strung with GHS Boomers, gauged .011–.056. I drop the sixth string to *C* and the fifth to *G*, which yields *C, G, D, G, B, E*. I use the same tuning a whole-step down [*B♭, F, C, F, A, D*] on my D-12, but I have unisons on the top four string pairs. Bending the wound third and fourth unison strings makes the D-12 sound like a bowed instrument."

An ambient guitar pioneer, the 47-year-old Tibbetts has been recording and mixing his own albums for more than two decades.

"Here's my sermon," he says. "Today, the average guitarist has access to better recording equipment than the Beatles used for *Rubber Soul*. It runs sideways to the financial interests of guitar magazines, but most people have enough gear. Instead of new toys, seek new adventures."

David Torn

BY MATT BLACKETT | MAY 2004

WE ALL KNOW WHAT IT MEANS WHEN A LIGHT BULB GOES
off over someone's head in a cartoon: A new idea is born. In the real world, capturing and recapturing that often elusive spark of invention is a draining, exasperating, and thrilling task. And, like gamblers pulling on the arms of slot machines, we always believe the next try will bring the big payoff.

David Torn is no stranger to this process. For more than three decades, he has cranked out unique music/noises/soundscapes as a guitarist, producer, sideman, and looping pioneer. His avant-garde, ambient, and futuristic stylings have attracted such diverse artists as k. d. lang, Bill Bruford, Jewel, Ryuichi Sakamoto, and David Bowie. Even pathologically creative musicians such as Jeff Beck have called on Torn to inject some life into tracks they felt they could take no further. He has lent his singular talents to several movie scores, sample CDs, and lots and lots of gigs. And at a time when the music industry is in the doldrums, Torn is busier than ever. Like a shark that will die if it stops moving, Torn is in constant creative motion—he even answers the phone by playing a searing cadenza. When he's not playing, mixing, or digitally vivisecting music, he's talking a blue streak, getting his ideas out at a frantic pace so his head doesn't explode.

Do you recall when you got that very first spark of, "Oh, my god—I'm on to something here"?

I was about 14, sitting by a campfire without a guitar in my hands. I became mesmerized by the fire. It was very quiet, and I just concentrated on the flames—how they moved, appeared, disappeared, and changed color. I started to hear a kind of music in my head based on the flames. There was this moment of personal revelation that allowed me to see a connection between how flames look when they're burning and how music sounds when it's very fluid. I went home the next day, and I realized I could translate this to the guitar.

You could translate that level of creative vision at 14?

Sort of. I found that if I stopped trying to copy what other people were playing, I could get closer to the vague goal of creating this flame music. That was the first real moment where I got that feeling of unfabricated expression. But as a guitarist, I would say that almost everything I've done since has been an attempt to regain that.

When are you at your best, creatively speaking?

When I'm not getting in my own way—whether that's with my chops or my harmonic vocabulary. If I think about super-cool chords or scales or some technique that seems "impressive," I usually fail creatively. It's the same with composing. When I don't give in to external agendas—like trying to copy someone or impress them—that's when I'm at my best. I generally don't like too much thinking or preplanning, although my *Cloud About Mercury* album was pretty strictly conceptualized and executed. It was strict but open at the same time, so the personalities of all the players still came through. With Splattercell, I felt I made a technological statement without losing the core of that "flame sound." I try to maintain an element of "nowness" with everything I do. I try to keep that raw edge—even if I'm writing parts for orchestral instruments.

It's as if you're applying improvisational concepts to nonimprovised music.

Well, I'm an improviser at heart, and that means I have to accept the really horrific things along with the beautiful things. I played a couple of gigs this week with [saxophonist] Tim Berne, [bassist] Fima Ephron, and [drummer] Ben Perowsky, and one of them was really terrible. You couldn't hear anything onstage, and we played like a bunch of idiots—except for Ben [*laughs*]. But then we had this amazing gig that was totally improvised. I had tunes to call, but I never got around to calling them, because what we were coming up with spontaneously felt so good. It was an incredibly satisfying, creative experience.

Many players are too afraid to go through the horrible gig to get to the beautiful one.

You have to get comfortable with the discomfort that goes along with the process. I'm addicted to the process—so much so that I no longer consider too deeply whether I've achieved my goal. The process is so satisfying that I really don't care what it sounds like. I have a recording of that great gig, for example, but I'm not interested in hearing it.

Really?

It's like sex. I am much more into the experience of having sex than I am in watching a video of it afterwards.

How does collaboration affect your creativity?

As a composer, there's always that egocentric thing where I like being in control. But as a player, I absolutely recognize I'm at my best when I'm communicating with other musicians. It can be an improvisational setting, and it can also be in the studio—like with Bowie's sessions, where there's a formatted tune and I'm the only one going off. There's still an interaction that is so critical for me.

What do you do when it's just not working? How do you get out of ruts?

If you really can't move forward with a song, then you have to move sideways. As a player, that means you have to move out of restrictive areas. You need to apply something to the piece of music that's outside the boundaries of what you already know. Re-tune the guitar to something you don't understand, or get a totally new tone. Sometimes, I have to pick up a different instrument—like the oud—and just play something. Even if it's bad, it might lead me somewhere, and it definitely leads me away from where I was. It helps if you look at music as a continuous path. Before you can arrive anywhere, you've got to travel.

"Before you can arrive anywhere, you've got to travel."

Let's say you've got a guitar, an oud, an Omnichord, an amp, and a looping device, and you have to create something out of nothing. Where do you begin?

I start with the guitar. From there, I'll almost always move to the looping device to form some shape to the music. I might just start with some odd noises, looping them and digitally chewing them up until that moment when inspiration kicks in. Then I'll grab the oud. That's a very creative instrument for me, because my skills are limited. I don't have a huge vocabulary to fall back on, and that makes it easier to write something fresh. After that, I'll get the Omnichord, find some chords that can sit with the oud part, and then process them heavily and loop them. At this point, I might throw all the tracks into the computer and start writing over the top of them. I have a lot of different paths I can take.

What are the benefits and drawbacks to having so much gadgetry at your disposal?

Well, first off, I don't look at anything as a gadget. I look at all these things as instruments. I use them as tools to build substance. So, in that sense, the benefits of having a huge toolbox are clear. Having a handle on effects, technology, instruments other than guitar, differently tuned guitars, other stringed instruments, little things you build—it's immeasurable what level of creativity can be sparked simply by changing instruments.

On the other hand, if you can't find anything substantial to say on any of these instruments, option anxiety can creep in. Then, jumping from one thing to another can be incredibly exhausting. When you're in that space, you have to shift gears. Choose one instrument, and just keep hammering away. When you're writing or creating, you have to work really hard to establish a flow.

What do you see as the biggest impediment to creativity these days?

I think the interest in all things retro has become a huge blockade for guitar-based music. Guitar playing in popular music is at its most conservative state right now. It used to be the instrument of the rebel. Now it's the instrument of dentists and accountants—although I don't mean to denigrate those occupations.

How can players break out of that?

There has to be a cutoff point where you stop copying guitarists or styles of music. You have to make an effort to get past your heroes and to get past this icon that the guitar has become. I mean, Jeff Beck continually progresses, but the guys who ape him are still living off *Wired* and *Blow by Blow*. Aside from Tom Morello, most of the current "guitar heroes" are not doing it for me. I love a good riff, but I want to hear some noise, I want to hear some new harmonic stuff, and I want some freaky technique that is unique to that player. It freaks me out that there isn't more room for expression. There is in the underground, and players like Raoul Bjorkenheim, Nels Cline, and Andre LaFosse are all doing amazing things. But in popular music, the guitar has lost its danger.

Most pop players are hesitant to go too far outside for fear of losing their gig.

Those players just need to look at themselves and ask, "How can I add something fresh and personal to this?" Even within the boundaries of pop music, I think you can use those boundaries as creative challenges. But you have to want that. Push it a little bit. Get beyond the idea that you can't play certain things because they're "incorrect."

It still sounds pretty scary.

Only if you stop. It gets easier if you just keep going. With any of your past work, look at it like, "That was great for then, but now I need the next step." We all need to believe that the next thing we do will be the best thing we've ever done. I'm never 100 percent satisfied with anything I've done in the past. And that's why I move forward.

James Blood Ulmer

BY JIMMY LESLIE | DECEMBER 2003

JAMES BLOOD ULMER IS CONCERNED WITH LITTLE ELSE but the truth. A disciple of Ornette Coleman's school of harmolodics, the avant-garde guitarist is best known for his unison-tuned free jazz excursions. But Ulmer's unassailable authenticity was a big influence on Living Color guitarist Vernon Reid, who came up with the idea of putting the crafty guitarist in a blues setting—which, amazingly, is one style Ulmer had not tackled.

In 2001, Reid took Ulmer to the sacred ground of Sun Studios—where Elvis, Carl Perkins, and Jerry Lee Lewis cut fabled tracks—to record *Memphis Blood: The Sun Sessions*. A collection of classic blues covers, the album won critical raves, but within a week of its release, the attacks of September 11 hit New York, leading to the quick demise of Ulmer's record label. Miraculously, a Grammy nomination for Best Traditional Blues Recording followed, bringing attention to the project and resulting in the album's reissue by Hyena records—as well as funding for the second chapter of the planned blues trilogy.

That chapter is *No Escape from the Blues: The Electric Lady Sessions*, which was tracked at Jimi Hendrix's dream studio in New York City. Reid decided that this episode would reflect the migration of the blues from its rural Southern roots to the urban centers of the North. Tunes like "Going to New York" and "Bright Lights,

Big City" also tell the story of Ulmer himself—a man who has lived the blues life for more than 60 years but only began recording it at the genesis of the millennium.

Was it difficult or strange adapting your style to the blues?

No, but that's because I don't think of the concept of blues as any one person's music. The concept of the blues is that everybody has something. It's about the stories you're telling—even though somebody might have told the story before. Muddy Waters and Howlin' Wolf weren't always singing their own songs. They were singing a lot of Willie Dixon's songs, but they were still expressing themselves. If you live the blues, you can express it. The blues is the soul of a man. You don't have to sound like anyone else.

> *"If you live the blues, you can express it."*

You have a very distinctive voice as a player and as a singer—how do you work both disciplines to best deliver a song?

Jimi Hendrix is the only person I know who could chew gum, smoke a cigarette, and sing and play the guitar. I can't focus like that. If I'm going to sing, I want to focus on singing. And when I'm going to play, it's a whole other thing that doesn't have anything to do with singing. You can't sing while I'm playing the guitar. You wouldn't be heard.

So what do you look for in an accompanist or coguitarist?

Well, I've had a few people sit in on my music before, and I really liked what Ronnie Drayton played because I don't know what it is or how he does it. Vernon is the same way. I'll be looking at his hands when he plays, and I still don't know what the hell he's doing [*laughs*]. I can deal with that, and it's actually what I like about other players. If I know what they're playing, why would I want to sit there and listen to it?

There are a lot of guitar sounds on the record. Can you identify which ones are yours and which ones are Vernon's?

I wound up playing my Gibson Byrdland. On one or two songs, we just miked it without plugging it in. I'd never done that before—it was Vernon's idea. I also plugged into a fuzz machine, so I've got about three or four guitar sounds on the record. The rest of the sounds are coming out of Vernon's guitar.

What subject comes up the most when you're talking guitar with Vernon?

We talk about living things. We don't actually talk about the instrument per se, because we are both experienced harmolodic players, and to be a harmolodic player, you have to understand what it means to be a harmolodic person. Harmolodics is a concept that everyone should explore.

Can you explain what it means to be a harmolodic person?

A harmolodic person is someone who can manifest himself in all kinds of different situations, whether it's playing blues, rock and roll, jazz, and so on. Whatever is going on in the American sound, he can participate on some level.

But let's say you got a jazz gig—wouldn't you need to have a specific jazz background and some experience with the genre?

A harmolodic person has to learn all of the American sounds, and jazz is a part of the American sound. But you don't really have to study it. You can learn how to play it by assimilation with people who know how to play it. I played with Art Blakey, Joe Henderson, and Ornette Coleman, and they're all jazz musicians.

How does a harmolodic person create art?

When you create the idea and then flow your art from your idea, then you are thinking harmolodically. You can say it's your art because you created the feel that you took the art from. Here's a good example of creating art harmolodically: I went to France, and this artist took us way out in the country where he had created this scene that he painted. He made the hills and the valleys, he planted flowers on the water, and he put the pond there in the first place. He created that landscape so he could paint it—which is what separates the concept of harmolodics from other concepts.

Interesting. Now can you explain the harmolodic concept as it pertains strictly to being a musician?

You would go out and learn every aspect of music before you call yourself a musician. You would be a musician because of a reason—not for no reason. You would be qualified to be what you are, because you are participating in all of the sounds of your land, and you would create music based on what you saw. You sow your seed, and then you reap your harvest. That's your art.

What does it mean to be a harmolodic player in terms of scales and chords? Don't they all go out the window?

A harmolodic player is different, but there are rules to playing harmolodically. I learned the rules from Ornette Coleman, and the rules are separate from the Western concept of playing. Scales and chords are eliminated in terms of the Western concept of what you use them for, and you don't use chords and scales in linear situations. All of your rhythm works off a concept that is superimposed on the linear concept. Everything goes in a circle. Nothing is linear. That's the harmolodic concept musically.

What is a harmolodic chord?

A harmolodic chord is a chord that cannot be inverted. Out of all the chords, there are only five that cannot be inverted, from which you can get major, minor, augmented, and diminished sounds.

Which five are those?

I don't want to get into it because it would take all day to discuss those five chords. I don't know how it goes on the piano or anything else, I only know how harmolodic chords work on the guitar. I can't say what they are, because to me they are only fingerings—voicings of intervals.

Do alternate tunings fit in with this concept?

You can play in standard, or you can use all kinds of tunings to fit whatever you want to do. I have what is called a "harmolodic tuning," where I tune all the strings in unison. This means that all six strings are tuned to the same note, and it can be any note. Then the drone of the guitar allows all 12 notes to be heard under that same note.

How do you apply the concept of harmolodics to the blues, which relies on its own formulas?

I just did the same thing that all blues players do, which is to accompany the song. If you are singing about a rooster, then you play rooster sounds on the guitar. If you're singing about a hound dog, then you try to sound like a hound dog. You play what is called the talking guitar—a call-and-response based on what you're singing about. You never try to turn into a guitarist. If you listen to the old blues records, they're about being a blues messenger, not a blues player.

Who were some of the urban blues players who influenced you?

I didn't have to listen to the blues—the blues was my life. For example, back when I was a boy, I didn't worry about listening to hillbilly music, because everything that came on the radio was hillbilly. I didn't have to study it, because it was already there in my face. I didn't have a record player then, and to this day, I don't have anybody's music in my house. I'm not allowed to listen to Muddy Waters and "take" his playing. I only listen to people for concept. Every band I ever played in was not about the music, it was about the concept. You don't have to play the music, you only need to play the concept of something. You don't have to know who a song was written by—it could be anybody's song based on anybody's experience—you just have to understand the concept.

It's interesting that you recorded "Are You Glad to Be in America?" again for this album.

Yes. I've recorded that song many times, and now I've got it in blues form. When I first made "Are You Glad to Be in America?," I was in England, and it was an underground English hit. That's how I got my recording contract with CBS. It's a big question, you know, and no American official wants to ask it, but I'm going to sing that song until they do. I'm waiting for President Bush to get on CSPAN and say to the nation,"Are you glad to be in America?"

What significance does the title of *No Escape from the Blues* have in regard to your life story?

Making a blues record is something I had been denying all of my life. I've been drawing from the blues all along, but my mother and father forbid me to play it because they were church people. So I would always shy away from playing blues straight up, and that's why I was learning other stuff. Finally Vernon came along with this blues idea, and I figured, I can't escape it, so I might as well stop trying to dodge it. It exists. This record is proof, so that's why I chose the title. Also, blues reveals the soul of a man, so you shouldn't be afraid to deal with the blues, because you will find out where your soul is at.

Jim Weider

BY ANDY ELLIS | JANUARY 2010

BEST KNOWN AS THE GUITARIST WHO REPLACED ROBBIE
Robertson in The Band, Jim Weider is hailed by many Telecaster aficionados as headmaster in the Roy Buchanan school of snarling blues. In addition to being The Band's guitarist for 15 years—a longer run than Robertson's—Weider has played and recorded with Bob Dylan, Los Lobos, Keith Richards, Dr. John, Taj Mahal, Mavis Staples, Paul Butterfield, rockabilly pioneers Scotty Moore and Paul Burlison, Bob Weir & RatDog, and Hot Tuna. Weider's Homespun instructional videos, including *Get That Classic Fender Sound!* and *Rockabilly Guitar*, reveal a deep knowledge of vintage gear and how early rockers used it.

Those familiar with Weider's rootsy musical past may be surprised to hear his new album, *Pulse*, which he recorded in three days with his band, Project Percolator. Featuring slamming drums and high-octane soloing, *Pulse* has a driving, psychedelic edge that veers between progressive rock and jam-band improv.

What led you to the rhythmic energy of *Pulse*?

This has been an evolutionary process that began a few years ago with my solo album, *Remedy*. I was trying to get into a groove area with that record but didn't quite make it. I felt I was writing myself into a corner, getting trapped by my blues-rock background. So, with the help of engineer and producer John Holbrook [Fountains of Wayne, Brian Setzer, B. B. King, Todd Rundgren, Mick Ronson], I went into my home studio and recorded a bunch of guitar instrumentals to electronic loops. Then

I got some great musicians—including drummer Rodney Holmes, John Medeski on organ, and Tony Levin on bass—to overdub and fill out the sound. This became *Percolator*, my first real groove-oriented album.

To perform that music, I put together a band with Rodney on drums, Steve Lucas on bass, and Mitch Stein on guitar. We've been gigging for a year or two. During that time we wrote the tunes you hear on *Pulse*. *Percolator* was more of a studio record, layered and built up through overdubs, whereas *Pulse* is how we sound live. We went into the studio—Mitch and I put our pedals on the floor and plugged into our stage amps—and just played. In three days we copped this record. There are a few overdubs—like where Mitch and I double the main riff in "No Exit Strategy"—but all the solos are live. These guys are all monster players, and it's a blast to have them as the bubble underneath my Tele.

Playing in The Band, you had two keyboardists—including the amazing Garth Hudson—providing harmonic color. Did you find it hard to adjust to Project Percolator's dual-guitar lineup?

Guitar Player readers know how much fun two guitarists can have in a band. Without keyboards, there's so much sonic space to explore. Mitch

"You've got to work a little harder on a Telecaster— relying on vibrato to get sustain, for example— and that defines your style."

plays a Strat, and his sound is a little darker and fatter. He also uses his effects—including a Line 6 DL4 delay and a Moogerfooger Ring Modulator—to create hip textures. Sometimes I'll crank up the repeats on my T-Rex Replica delay and play some swirling slide notes while Mitch works his Moogerfooger, and we'll get into an atmospheric jam that takes me back to my psychedelic days.

In sections of "Green Zone," your guitar parts sound like sequenced keyboard lines.

Ai-yi-yi—*that* tune! Mitch played the low part and I played the high part as an overdub. My solo is live, and you can see me track it in a video we have on our site [jimweider.com]. I just plugged in and went for it while they filmed that take. I was really happy—the solo felt right and the tone was killin'.

What was your rig for "Green Zone"?

I played my '52 Tele through an AnalogMan King of Tone pedal—an overdrive I codesigned with Mike Piera—and an old Vox wah into my signature Fargen JW-40 head. I ran through a vintage Marshall basketweave 4x12 cabinet that belonged to the studio. It sounded *perfect*. For years I've played through Fender amps, but recently I discovered how great a Tele sounds through a Fender-style head and Marshall 4x12. I have an old Marshall 4x12 with late-'60s Celestion greenbacks, but I only bring it to big shows where I have help to lift it. I should have been playing a 4x12 all those years I was in The Band and had roadies!

Tell us about your '52 Tele.

I've always played Teles—I bought them at Manny's in the '60s—but once I heard Roy Buchanan playing a '50s Tele with a flat-pole bridge pickup, I wanted *that* sound. So I went on a search and finally found a '50s Tele in L.A. in 1971. I've been playing it ever since. It's on every Band record I've played on, as well as every track on *Pulse*, except for "Man Cry"—the slide song in open *E* minor tuning [*E*, *B*, *E*, *G*, *B*, *E*, low to high]. For that tune I used a Tele retrofitted with an old Supro pickup, like Ry Cooder's guitar.

My '52 has the original bridge pickup, but Dominick Ramos rewound the neck pickup with longer magnets and it's still the best-sounding one I've come across. I'm playing through that pickup on "Talking with You."

What's so special about '50s Telecasters?

The flat-pole magnets in the bridge pickup allow you to raise it closer to the strings for a fat, almost compressed sound that has bite but also some balls and bottom. With flat magnets, your *G* string is not twice as loud as your *B* string. The pickup has a more even string-to-string response—that's the sound of the '50s. To get more girth in each note I've got my bridge pickup raised as high as it can go without hitting the strings. Same with the neck pickup. You don't have that Strat problem, where the strings are pulled out of tune when the pickups are too close.

Do you have other vintage Teles?

I also have a '53 and '54, both with flat-pole bridge pickups. All three guitars sound a little different—the fattest is my '52—so if you're hunting for a vintage Tele, you have to take your time. I like the '52 and '53 neck profile, which is a soft V. My '52 neck is smaller than my '53 and '54. For some reason, in '52 they made the necks a little thinner, and I got used to that. To get the most out of a '50s Tele, you've got to set them up right, which includes installing bigger frets—a trick I learned from Roy Buchanan. It makes a Tele play better and you can bend strings a lot easier.

What kind of fretwire do you use?

For years on my '52 Tele I've been using Dunlop 6100 fretwire. It measures .110" wide and .055" high—that's really tall. I get my repairman to mill the frets down to .050", which he grudgingly does. Because he can just put it in, he prefers another fretwire sold by Stewart-MacDonald that measures .100" by .050" [Stew-Mac's Wide/High fretwire]. I lean toward the wider size, but I want to start with at least a .050" height, because by the time you round off the frets so they bend like butter, they're .048" high. I don't want to go any lower than that. I'm always bending two or three strings and I play really hard, so I have to refret regularly.

I replace my pots a lot too, because I'm working my tone and volume control all the time—something else I learned from Roy. I use RS Guitarworks pots with solid brass shafts.

Do you play any modern Teles?

Fender sent me a Road Worn Tele, which James Pennebaker—their Artist Relations guy in Nashville—picked out for me. It has big frets, and all the lacquer is rubbed off the back of the neck like on my old Teles. The Custom Shop installed a set of '51 Nocaster pickups, and they really sound good. The neck profile is right on, and even though the fretboard has a tight 7.25" radius, the frets are tall enough you can bend strings easily. It's one of the nicest guitars you can buy that's playable off the rack. I'm using it onstage with [The Band's iconic drummer] Levon Helm and also with Project Percolator.

What about strings, picks, and slides?

I've been using Dunlop 215 glass slides for years. I prefer the sweet sound of glass to chrome or brass. The 215 is light enough you can get away with low action, which means it works well for playing slide on a Tele in standard tuning—my usual approach. I use Ernie Ball strings, gauged .010–.048, and a small, extra-heavy, jazz-style Fender flatpick. I use a hybrid pick-and-fingers technique with a little bit of nail combined with the fingertip.

How did Roy Buchanan inspire you?

The moment I heard "Sweet Dreams" [the opening track on 1972's *Roy Buchanan*], I totally got it. I was knocked out by the sounds he could get by cranking the amp and then just manipulating his Tele's volume and tone controls. To this day, his *Second Album* has some of the best Tele tones I've ever heard.

The first time I saw Roy was in the early '70s, and he was at the top of his game. He was playing Nancy, his blonde Tele, through two cranked Fender Vibrolux combos. It was *unbelievably* great. How you touch a Tele has so much to do with the tones you get out of it, and Roy's touch was magical. Jesse Ed Davis was another Tele player who blew me away with his touch, string bending, and vibrato. I just went crazy about those early Taj Mahal records that featured Jesse Ed [*Taj Mahal*, *The Natch'l Blues*, and *Giant Step*].

Did you ever play with Buchanan?

The Band played with Roy right before he went down. We did "Hand Jive"—it was great. He could take a harmonic and bend it way up in the middle of a solo and just blow your mind. I asked him, "Did you teach Robbie Robertson how to play pinch harmonics?" He said, "Well, yes, but I taught him the *wrong* way." That was funny. Roy was really secretive.

All these years, you've stuck with a Tele—why?

You've got to work a little harder on a Telecaster—relying on vibrato to get sustain, for example—and that defines your style. Half the time you're struggling to get a sound from your instrument, and that makes what you play more interesting.

James Williamson

BY MICHAEL MOLENDA |
GUITARPLAYER.COM, JANUARY 2010

JAMES WILLIAMSON'S KICK-ASS COOL, STREET-THUG GUITAR
cacophony was the jet engine of the Stooges' classic and influential *Raw Power* album in 1973. Then he channeled the same aggro-punk vibe—though in a spookier
direction—for the chilling demo tracks that were ultimately released as his and Iggy
Pop's "solo project," *Kill City*, in 1977. It was a shock, then, around 1980, when
this most feral of guitarists chucked his music career to get an electrical engineer-
ing degree and go to work for Sony. Williamson stayed pretty much out of the rock
biz, until the tragic and untimely death of Stooges guitarist Ron Asheton in 2009
prompted him to take early retirement from Sony and rejoin the band. In 2010, the
Stooges were inducted into the Rock and Roll Hall of Fame.

Are you still playing a Les Paul with the Stooges?

Right now, I'm playing three guitars: my original Les Paul Custom, a Collings 290,
and a Fender Stratocaster for the old stuff. It's still in flux, though. I'm making a replica of my Les Paul, because I don't want the original beat up on the road. I'm also
toying with playing two Les Pauls, but I love the Collings, so I may keep it in the mix.

What about amps?

I'm kind of a Vox and Marshall guy from way back when, but the sound on my records has been largely Vox—a Vox amp with a Les Paul plugged into it. Now, however, I'm using Blackstar amps, because the first channel is basically a Vox AC30—which I liked right away—but you get more tonal and textural control.

Do you set your amp controls in any particular way?

For the most part, I crank the volume, boost the treble, and have at it. The sound isn't really distorted and muddy, because I like to be able to hear the music. So my overdrive sound is pretty edgy and cutting.

"It's really that simple. I just played what felt right to me, and suddenly I had a style that people seemed to like."

Any pedals?

I've always played pretty much straight through—no pedals. Lately, however, I've been using a boost pedal just to get a bit more sustain for solos. Also, I've started using a wah pedal to represent the songs from the first couple of albums more accurately.

Even when you plug straight in, there's a wonderful feral vibe to your playing. It sounds like there's more going on than there is.

Yeah. It's hard to describe. But the only real secret to playing my songs, boys and girls, is to use downstrokes almost exclusively. My picks are imprinted: "Shortest Distance Between Two Chords." Now, if you do that right—play the right chords with a Les Paul and some humbuckers—then you'll be a lot closer. Get a Vox or a Blackstar amp, and you're going to be *very* close.

Do you ever mess with the guitar's Volume and Tone controls?

It depends on the song. If I'm playing something with more dynamics—like "Gimme Danger" or "Open Up and Bleed"—I'll use the neck pickup for most of the song and then go to the bridge pickup, or perhaps I'll take the guitar Volume down a bit so that the sound isn't so distorted. Obviously, for solos I go full out using the bridge pickup. Most everything else is bridge pickup, as well.

How did you develop your own style?

I listened to a lot of guys, but I developed my own style because it was easier for me to do my own stuff than to try to play somebody else's. It's really that simple. I just played what felt right to me, and suddenly I had a style that people seemed to like. So there were really no specific influences, although my big hero of all time—and still is—is Jeff Beck. I knew I couldn't play like him, though, so I just did what I do.

Like Beck, you do very vocal-esque bends.

Yeah. Well, he's the master. How he works a whammy bar to get all those vocal cries and everything is amazing. I don't use whammy bars, so I had to figure out how to do that stuff with my fingers. I don't think about it much—I just get into it.

Lyle Workman

BY MATT BLACKETT | AUGUST 2009

LYLE WORKMAN IS SOMETHING OF A MULTITASKER. OR HE'S schizophrenic. Or maybe he just can't say no. How else can you explain a career path that has taken him from pop funksters Bourgeois Tagg to playing wingman for Todd Rundgren to sessions and gigs for Jellyfish, Beck, Frank Black, Sting, and many others? And that doesn't take into account his most high-profile work over the past few years: scoring smash-hit movies such as *40-Year-Old Virgin*, *Superbad*, and *Forgetting Sarah Marshall*.

But that still ain't all. There's the Lyle Workman we see here. The guy who releases elaborate, intricate solo albums where he combines complex string and percussion arrangements with massive guitar layers and textures and chops that call to mind Jimmy Page, John McLaughlin, and Jeff Beck. That's what listeners are treated to on Workman's latest, *Harmonic Crusader*, a record that features tons of his guitar work but also the drumming of monsters such as Simon Phillips, Gary Novak, and Vinnie Colaiuta.

How did you find the time to make this record?

I worked on it on and off for about eight years, in between touring and movies. Basically in between all of my income.

What was the evolution of the songs, from the writing stage to the demos to the finished product?

Some songs were written and recorded in a very short period of time. For example, most of the song "Ode to the Gypsy King" was done in a few days. And

"Devotion" came together pretty much in one day. It's essentially just one acoustic guitar, one electric guitar, and my voice. I played a really old Washburn parlor-sized gut-string guitar from the 1800s and overdubbed the second half with my '72 Thinline Tele through my '66 Fender Princeton.

"Ruckus Maximus" was a tune that took a long time to finish. It required a lot of work to embellish it the way I wanted, and I didn't have enough time to do it start to finish when I wrote it. I basically fleshed the whole thing out—the chord progression and the melodies—with just one guitar and a click. Then I started to add instruments like drums and bass. That song has Simon Phillips on drums. When I came up with the A section, I just heard Simon playing it. I had him in the back of my mind, because I had been listening to all those Jeff Beck records.

That tune has some pretty wild lead work.

I believe the solos on that song were tracked to a click. My plan the entire time was to replace the solos. But there's something about the relaxed state I'm in when I know it's not for real, when I know I'm going to come back to it and replace it. There's an ease to my playing. I'm not too precious about it, and that's what happened there. When I listened back after Simon played on it, I ended up keeping my rough solo.

What kind of direction did you give him on the track?

I sent him an mp3 of the basic version and a chart, because there were several meter changes. I didn't know how he was going to feel some of the sections, because they can be felt a couple of different ways. If you were to listen to this song with a click track, you might be surprised where the click is.

Like a lot of tunes on this record, the guitar on "Ruckus Maximus" is doubled with other instruments. Talk about your approach to those layers.

That doubling usually happens toward the end of recording. Once I outline the basic harmony and outfit it with the meat and potatoes guitar, then I'm always looking for textures that I can add to give it some variety. On that song, there's a guitar melody that's being doubled by vibes and marimba—sort of a Frank Zappa-style thing. I wrote all the notes out for the percussionists, and it's a fairly elaborate chart, with some of the notes flying by pretty quickly. I love the sound of guitar being doubled by percussive instruments like vibes. I also love the sound of guitar and strings, and there's a fair amount of that on this record, as well. I'm a huge fan of classical music, where you've got brass, strings, horns, and woodwinds. Within that framework you can get a lot of textures, and I like to apply that concept to the music I write. I'm always into a wider sonic scope than what electric guitar, bass, keyboards, and drums can provide, even though a lot of great music has been written with that instrumentation.

At about 5:00 in "Burning of the Brightest Flame," there's a really fast, intricate passage that kind of sounds like guitar but kind of doesn't.

I'm doubling that line in octaves. That was my modified 1969 100-watt Marshall that I just love the sound of. I use that a lot.

What other gear did you rely on?

I used a lot of Divided by 13 amps. On the guitar front, I played my '63 Strat, a '58 reissue Les Paul, and my '72 Thinline Tele—a lot of the lush chordal stuff is that guitar. I miked the amps with a Shure SM57 and either a Royer R-121 ribbon or this Heil PR30 that I really like on guitars. I tend to use those microphones in combination, and I blend them pretty much half and half.

"Pieds-en-l'Air" has some incredible EBow work. How did you put that together?

Dave Gregory from XTC told me about this composer, Peter Warlock, who wrote a piece called "Capriol Suite." I got the CD and there was this one movement, "Pieds-en-l'Air," that I just loved. I got the score and recorded the parts one by one with an EBow. Then I tripled or quadrupled each track to give it the sound of a guitar orchestra. That's 21 tracks of EBow guitar.

"I'm relying on my ears and my abilities, and I'm constantly surprising myself with things."

Did you take steps to make certain parts sound more like clarinets, oboes, or cellos?

I did. For the cello parts, I didn't want such a vibrant top end, so I rolled the tone off the guitar a bit and changed the EQ on the amp. I wanted to give each part its own space as much as I could.

Your resume is pretty varied. Was there a guitarist that you modeled your career path after?

No. I don't know if it's because I get bored easily or that I have an interest in all aspects of music, but any time I was anywhere near an opportunity, if I was asked, I would just say yes, even if I didn't know what I was doing. Yes, yes, yes. I'm doing orchestral stuff for films now. I don't have any background in that. I'm relying on my ears and my abilities, and I'm constantly surprising myself with things. It's amazing how much you can do that you never knew you could do.

Dave Wronski

BY DARRIN FOX | APRIL 2000

FOR SLACKTONE'S DAVE WRONSKI, THE MAIN INGREDIENT
to kick-ass surf music is a no-nonsense approach.

"Keep the music as simple as possible and get to the point," he says. "Listen to the first Police, Van Halen, or Ramones albums. Even though they're not surf, those records give you just the essentials, and they're very urgent sounding."

Slacktone's self-titled debut shows off the group's ability to keep the restlessness of traditional surf without resorting to clichés. While "Tidal Wave" is a tsunami of surf-approved low-string melodies and power-chord angst, the album also flaunts Slacktone's prowess at applying a romantic element to the genre. On "Nocturne," for example, Wronski states the tune's

> *"Keep the music as simple as possible and get to the point."*

reflective melody while interspersing haunting, delicately vibratoed chords over the rhythm section.

"I don't really think of myself as a surf guitarist," he says. "I've played all types of music in my life, and to me it's all related. Mixing moods can also make an album or live set feel like a theme-park ride."

For Slacktone, Wronski used a vintage multiamp setup: a '64 Super Reverb, a tweed Bassman, a Vox AC30, a '55 Fender Princeton, and a plexi Marshall. To play through all five amps simultaneously, Wronski split the signal from his '58 Strat—one side went to a tube Echoplex and Fender reverb unit and was then routed to three amps; the other side went to another tube Echoplex and Fender reverb that fed the remaining two amps. The amps were miked individually and recorded on separate tracks.

"This setup allowed me to track live—no overdubs—and still get a huge sound," says Wronski. "And even though it's a clean guitar tone, it comes on pretty strong."

To Wronski, surf music's most appealing quality is its instantly identifiable sound. "Everyone understands the vibe and likes it—it communicates very well," he explains. "At a party, if someone picks up a guitar and plays 'Walk, Don't Run' everybody digs it. If I can add anything to that world of instrumental rock guitar, then I'm on the right track."

Jimmy Wyble

AS TOLD TO FRANKIE R. NEMKO | JUNE 1977

SOFT-SPOKEN, HUMBLE JIMMY WYBLE—BORN IN PORT ARTHUR,
Texas, in 1922—has compiled a resume equally impressive in both country and jazz circles. Joining Bob Wills and His Texas Playboys in 1944, Jimmy would often spice up the western dance numbers by adding Charlie Christian or Django Reinhardt lines to his solos.

The Wills band eventually brought Wyble to California, where he came in contact with more jazz and studio guitarists. A short stint with Spade Cooley's country group preceded Jimmy's full-fledged induction into the jazz world when he joined vibist Red Norvo's combo in the mid-'50s. Wyble played with Norvo for eight years, during which time he also accompanied Frank Sinatra and toured with Benny Goodman. In 1964, when his wife took ill, Jimmy decided to stay in Los Angeles and work in the studios. He played on numerous recordings, television shows, and soundtracks such as Ocean's 11 *and* The Wild Bunch.

"Where I grew up there were a whole lot of guitarists on the block, so to speak—no organized combos, just dozens of fiddle bands. We'd sometimes drive a couple of hundred miles for a dance and make a buck for the night! But we all loved to play so much it was worth it.

"Even though I was occupied with country and western music for a living, all the time I was also listening to such people as [jazz violinist] Joe Venuti and [guitarist] Eddie Lang. I remember hearing [clarinetist] Benny Goodman on the radio and the Red Norvo/Mildred Bailey band, never dreaming that one day I'd be playing with

them! I'd send away for every guitar book I heard about and would spend labori-
ous hours picking a measure here and there. I learned the Alan Reuss solos but was
never really able to handle that kind of material at that time.

"I was utterly amazed when I first heard Django Reinhardt on records. For a
short time, being such a novice, I actually tried to copy a few bars here and there,
which was quite ridiculous, because at that point I had absolutely no proficiency.
Then I heard Charlie Christian, and I was totally devastated. Not that I considered
Charlie better than Django—it was just something that happened to me emotionally
whenever I'd listen to Charlie play. I spent as many hours as possible trying to learn
some of his licks.

"There was another guitarist in the Bob Wills band at the same time I was named
Cameron Hill, who, like me, was an allout fan of Charlie Christian. Cameron would
copy a chorus of, say, Charlie's 'Flying Home,' and he and I would play it in harmony. Bob used to refer to us as 'twin guitars.' That was the good thing about Bob,
he didn't restrict us to playing in the country style. Whatever we could bring to the
job, he'd let us do. Some of us who were really into listening to jazz would take some
incredible solos right in the middle of all that cowboy stuff! That was a very swinging
band. In those days, we were often referred to as the country and western version
of the Benny Goodman group. Bob really knew nothing about music, but he was
such an emotional inspiration to all of us in the band, and that alone made us cook.

"Those early experiences in the studio with Bob Wills meant so much to me in
terms of meeting the likes of George Smith, George Van Eps, and Barney Kessel.
Also during that time, we'd be playing at these huge ballrooms for up to 7,000 people, and right next door at a smaller jazz place would be someone like [trumpeter]
Harry James or [saxophonist] Charlie Barnet. That's how I got to meet so many of
the jazz greats and become so influenced by them.

"When I decided to stay in Los Angeles, I was still working with a country and
western band. However, Spade Cooley ran a much tighter ship than Bob Wills. He
was far more rigid and stuck pretty faithfully to the country and western concepts.
It's curious to me now how working in such an atmosphere I always somehow managed to be taken into areas where I'd meet the jazz people. Like [reed player] Jimmy
Giuffre. He and Barney Kessel were on the faculty at the American Operatic Lab in
L.A., so I went there for a while and studied with them.

"My ambition was really never anything other than to play guitar. I didn't even
know what a studio guitarist was, much less a whole orchestra of guitars. I just had a
burning desire to play, no matter how or where. But in the 1950s, I was listening to
Tal Farlow, who at that time was with Red Norvo at the Haig Club in Hollywood. I
used to go and listen to them, and that became quite a turning point for me. When

Tal left Red for a few months, he was replaced by Jimmy Raney. Once again, I'd sit in front of the band all night long, absorbing every note that Jimmy played. This was also around the time Jim Hall was playing with [percussionist] Chico Hamilton when [flute and reed player] Buddy Collette and [cellist] Fred Katz were in the group. I was learning so much from all those guys. And it was during that period that I first met Tony Rizzi, who was just so far ahead of the game then.

"Those years were very important to me, because after Tal left Red Norvo in 1956, a young guitarist named Bill Dillard joined Red and made two albums with the group. We were close friends and jammed a lot. Then Bill was tragically killed in a fire, and Red asked me to take over Bill's chair. I was absolutely overwhelmed. My reply was, 'I'd like to, but I can't play like Tal or Jimmy or Bill.' Red told me, 'I'm not interested in that. All I'm concerned with is whether you're interested in growing and learning.'

"I have to confess here and now that Red Norvo literally saved my life. At that point, I had become a thoroughly, emotionally, frustrated, mixed-up person—to the degree of becoming an alcoholic. What a task for anyone to undertake. Here was this young, inexperienced, emotionally disturbed musician, and Red virtually taught me how to function in his wonderful trio and quintet. So, in addition to what I gained musically—which was vast, believe me—just learning to accept myself, and making an honest effort was all attributable to Red Norvo.

"I stayed with Red for eight years, traveling extensively throughout the U.S. and abroad. In 1964, the band went to Australia, where we accompanied Frank Sinatra. During that period with Red, I was fortunate to have the opportunity to take part in several tours with Benny Goodman, as well, and record with his orchestra.

"So you can see my musical life was taking on a very different look and sound. Before I joined Red—and after I had gotten to hear all those guitar greats like Charlie Christian, Barney Kessel, Herb Ellis, and numerous others—I became bent on playing like them. I was just obsessed by the need to copy my idols. Coming under Red's influence at the age of 35, 1 found myself being awakened for the first time to the fact that we have to grow as individuals. I learned that even if I'd had the proficiency to emulate those idols, it wouldn't have been the right thing to do.

"The last time I officially worked with Red's group was in 1964. And it has been since then, really, that I've become more and more involved in the studios, playing on numerous television shows, record dates, and movie scores. Probably one of the most exciting projects I ever had in the studios was with Laurindo Almeida. He had written a score for three guitars, so Laurindo played classical, I was on electric, and Bobby Bain handled the bass guitar.

"I gradually developed my own style and approach to studio work, and I began experimenting with different kinds of instruments. When I first arrived in Los Angeles way back in 1944, I had just one guitar—the Guild Johnny Smith Artist Award model. I had met Johnny in Denver, fell in love with his sound, and decided I had to have that for myself. But as soon as I began freelancing, I realized I had to get into the electric instrument, so I got myself a Fender. Incidentally, when I was with one of those cowboy bands, Leo Fender came and gave each of us guitarists one of his very first Telecasters—which he made practically in his garage. I still have it, and I occasionally play it on a record date or something.

"I also knew that I'd need a lot of gadgets in studio work, so I got a Fender amp, a wah-wah pedal, fuzzboxes, and an Electro-Harmonix Small Stone phaser. I must admit in all honesty, though, that I'm not that much into rock playing. I use all these accoutrements from time to time, but I'm really not that adept at the new music. I mostly enjoy playing my acoustic guitars. I have a 6- and a 12-string, a Martin flattop, a Howard Roberts jazz model, and a custom-made Guild Mark 7 classical instrument.

"I finally gave up my Fender amp and bought a Benson 300 amp. Now, I have an early vintage Polytone 102 amp—which I use almost exclusively for jazz—and a Polytone Mini Brute.

"Another instrument—a new innovation that I'm just getting to know—is the Guitorgan. It's made by a company in Texas called MusiConics International. Basically, it's like a Hammond B-3 organ built inside an electric guitar. It's played the same way as guitar, with no difference in tuning or in the fingerboard. However, there is a preciseness that's *really* required in the left hand. In playing guitar, you can anticipate the note, and it doesn't play until you actually pluck that string. However, with the organ attachment, as soon as a string makes contact with the fret, it's playing that note. You can't accidentally bump into things. I would say that for a good technical player it would present no problems. In fact, it would force a person to play correctly.

"I was involved in Tony Rizzi's Five Guitars right from the very beginning, and it has been a tremendous experience. Playing with Tony after all these years of admiring him so much is like a dream come true—a great privilege. As *Guitar Player* readers probably know, Tony has taken those early, recorded solos by our mutual idol Charlie Christian and harmonized them for five guitars. The challenge involved in playing those charts really keeps me on my toes.

"I firmly believe that the whole music scene is changing so much now that someday very soon Tony's contribution to the guitar world will be available in schools for ensemble playing. When I first started out, I didn't have the opportunities to be exposed to such things. In fact, I was never formally trained in music. I did take a few lessons from a man named Raymond Jones—a machinist who was also an avid guitarist. He's a fine craftsman, and he is still building beautiful guitars. He taught me the rudiments of reading and the first legitimate aspects of playing guitars. He took me through the Nick Lucas and Nick Manoloff books.

"Now I'm involved in teaching. Since the advent of my first published book, *Classical/Country*, I've been virtually forced into teaching. The material in the book isn't really country or classical, but because of my background, it cuts across all the lines—classical, country, jazz. The basic concept involves a two-line contrapuntal approach, creating pianistic sounds on the guitar. I've been asked to demonstrate and speak about this innovation at such prestigious places as Lee Ritenour's Master Guitar class at USC and Dick Grove's Workshop in North Hollywood. I'm also passing it on to some of my private students who are interested in this form. My involvement with the contrapuntal writing has become almost an obsession, but I can see great potential. It could quite easily lead to being able to improvise with two lines instead of one.

"My ambition was really never anything other than to play guitar."

"Today, my heroes are many. Of course, Jimi Hendrix was a tremendous innovator and stylist, and we always need to have those kinds of people in any art form. None of us could help but be influenced in some way by his contribution. I really like to listen to all the new people, like Eric Clapton, Robben Ford, Lee Ritenour, Tim May and Mike Rosati [both with Tony Rizzi's group], and Jay Graydon, who did the *Andy Williams Show* with me. You'll be hearing a lot more of him. All the people in the rock scene—so many of them have tremendous musicianship and taste. I also have the greatest admiration for some of the studio guitarists, like Tommy Tedesco, Mike Anthony, and, of course, Howard Roberts—who, by the way, was very helpful in the publication of my books.

"I do want to stress, though, that the greatest lesson I have learned over the years is to not become so completely enraptured by certain heroes that your playing is exactly like theirs, because that could turn out to be a stumbling block—a dead end. I'm so glad that my experiences have broadened my horizons. There's just so much variety in music today. The resources are endless."